NEW WORLD WISDOM
Book One

ALSO BY LORI TOYE

A Teacher Appears

Sisters of the Flame

Fields of Light

The Ever Present Now

New World Wisdom Series

Points of Perception

Light of Awakening

Divine Destiny

Freedom Star Book

I AM America Map

Freedom Star Map

6-Map Scenario

US Golden City Map

New World *Wisdom*

Teachings from the Ascended Masters

Book One

LORI ADAILE TOYE

 I AM AMERICA PUBLISHING & DISTRIBUTING
P.O. Box 2511, Payson, Arizona, 85547, USA.
www.iamamerica.com

© (Copyright) 2016 by Lori Adaile Toye. All rights reserved.
ISBN: 978-1-880050-53-8

All rights exclusively reserved, including under the Berne Convention and the Universal Copyright Convention. No part of this book may be reproduced or translated in any language or utilized in any form or by any means, electronic or mechanical, including photocopying, recording, or by any information storage and retrieval system, without written permission from the publisher. Published in 2014 by I AM America Seventh Ray Publishing International, P.O. Box 2511, Payson, Arizona, 85547, United States of America.

I AM America Maps and Books have been marketed since 1989 by I AM America Seventh Ray Publishing and Distributing, through workshops, conferences, and numerous bookstores in the United States and internationally. If you are interested in obtaining information on available releases please write or call:
I AM America, P.O. Box 2511, Payson, Arizona, 85547, USA. (928) 978-6435, or visit:

www.iamamerica.com
www.loritoye.com
www.loritoye.org

Graphic Design and Typography by Lori Toye
Editing by Dorothy Maville, Elaine Cardall, Betsy Robinson

Love, in service, breathes the breath for all!
Print On Demand Version
10 9 8 7 6 5 4 3 2 1

> "*Do you feel the movement of your soul into a different reality?*"
>
> ~ KUTHUMI

Contents

FOREWORD	XXI
PREFACE	XXIII
ABOUT THE I AM AMERICA MAPS	XXX

CHAPTER ONE

Opening • 35

Appearance of Saint Germain 37
Four White-Robed Beings Unroll a Map 37
Ascended Masters and the Christ Consciousness 40

CHAPTER TWO

Beginning Notes • 43

Genesis of the Golden Cities 44

CHAPTER THREE

Golden Crystal Age • 47

Ascension Valley 47
The Cascade Mountains 48
Mount Shasta 49

CHAPTER FOUR

Meteorites • 51

Oregon 51

CHAPTER FIVE
Golden Cities ♦ 53
Golden Cities of the Western United States 53
Mississippi River 54
Continental Divide 55

CHAPTER SIX
Structure ♦ 59
The Mountain of Light 59
Washington, DC 61

CHAPTER SEVEN
Coastlines ♦ 63
Washington State 63
Melting Ice and the New Magnetic North 64

CHAPTER EIGHT
Five Stars ♦ 65
The Great Lakes 65
The Five New Regions of the United States 69

CHAPTER NINE
Golden Names ♦ 71
A Global, Cultural Consciousness 71

CHAPTER TEN
Fertile Valley ♦ 75
New Orleans 76
Unites States: New Agricultural Areas
and Transportation Routes 77

Weather Changes................................78
The United States West Coast 79
Spiritual Protection 81

CHAPTER ELEVEN
Refinement ✦ 85

The United States East Coast.....................86

CHAPTER TWELVE
From the Heart ✦ 91

A Spiritual Technique to Aid Manifestation..........91

CHAPTER THIRTEEN
Choice ✦ 93

The Cleansing and the Law of Attraction 93
Higher Vibration, Love, and Forgiveness 94
Sustaining Love through the Practice
of the Violet Flame..............................96
Choice Reflects Our True Motivations 98
The Natural Law of Responsibility 100

CHAPTER FOURTEEN
With Love ✦ 103

Journey Into the Seventh Cycle...................103
Prophecy, Fear, and the Dimension of Love 105
Baja, Mexico....................................106
The Yucatan....................................108

CHAPTER FIFTEEN
Dance of the Circle • 109

The Elemental Life of Fourth Dimension............109
Volcanic Activity................................111
The Time of Transition..........................113

CHAPTER SIXTEEN
Heartland • 115

The Process of Becoming.........................115
Flame of Freedom 119
The Mother's Heart and the First Race 120
Deep Within Self and the Lake of Mirrors........121
Central America.................................122
Reappearance of the Master 124

CHAPTER SEVENTEEN
Trust • 127

Beyond Duality and the I AM Presence 128
Trust the Presence 128

CHAPTER EIGHTEEN
Loving Prayer • 131

You are ONE with the Earth......................132
Detach from Ego through the Divine Will.........134
Oneness and Divine Love 136
Earth Cleansing and the New Dimensions
  of Consciousness..............................137

CHAPTER NINETEEN
Cradleland • 139

The Andes Mountains..........................139
Balance and the New Economy..................141
Brazil.......................................142
Rio de Janerio...............................144
The Golden Cities of Central America 145
The Spiritual Vibration of the I AM America Maps...145
Accept the Gift..............................147

CHAPTER TWENTY
Everno • 151

Mother Mary 152
A Dimension Beyond Cause and Effect............154
Cuba...155
The Trinity of Love, Wisdom, and Power..........156
A Timeless Heart 157

CHAPTER TWENTY-ONE
Bay of the Golden Sun • 159

The Gulf of Mexico 159
Golden Waters and Glacial Flows 161
Ice Sheets...................................163
The Amethyst City............................165
The Rise of the Wisdom Schools of Ascension 166

CHAPTER TWENTY-TWO
Open Doors ◆ 169

Personal Choices Sculpt Your Destiny 169
The Golden Cities of South America. 171
The Christed Leaders of the New Times 172

CHAPTER TWENTY-THREE
White Dove ◆ 173

Love is an Action 173
White Dove Island 176

CHAPTER TWENTY-FOUR
Expansive Completion ◆ 179

Completion Engenders an Expansive Beginning 179
The Rythmic, Creative Wave 181
Love One Another 183

CHAPTER TWENTY-FIVE
Harmony: The Law of Agreement ◆ 187

Earth Changes and the Spiritual Hierarchy 187
We are All in this Together 189
Harmony Maintains Balance 190
The Consciousness of Minerals and Crystals. 192
The Harmonic Flow of Sound .193

CHAPTER TWENTY-SIX
Abundance: The Law of Choice ◆ 195

Akashic Records. 196
Abundance is the Natural Result of Harmony 197
Same Vibration Equals Agreement. 199

The Difference between Prosperity and
Abundance..................................201

CHAPTER TWENTY-SEVEN
Clarity: The Law of Non-judgment ◆ 205
What is the Light?............................207
Apply Each Jurisdiction in Sequence,
One at a Time 207
Everyone is of the Light 211

CHAPTER TWENTY-EIGHT
Love: The Law of Allowing, ◆ 213
Maintaining, and Sustainability
Allowing Sustains and Nurtures Love 215
Feminine Love Maintains, the Male Sustains 216
Masculine Love Sustains and Protects..............216
Love and Creation 217
Beyond Love's Passion: Tolerance and Agreement ...219
The Purpose of the Jurisdictions..................220
Our Precious Time on Earth.....................221

CHAPTER TWENTY-NINE
Service: The Law of Love ◆ 223
Service Releases Power..........................224
Give without Expectation........................224
Service is an Expression of Love 226
Share from Your Heart..........................227
Service is Multi-faceted and Has
Multiple Expressions 229

CHAPTER THIRTY
Illumination: Live without Fear or Judgment • 233
"BE" with Knowing and Non-judgment............233
A Mind without Fear..........................234
The Illumined Mind Works for the ONE............236

CHAPTER THIRTY-ONE
Cooperation: Live with Beauty and Honor • 239
See Beauty in All Things.......................240
Cooperation...................................240
About Doubt and Judgment......................242

CHAPTER THIRTY-TWO
Cooperation: Honor Your Divinity • 245
Cooperation is both Part and Whole 245
Immortal, Timeless Divinity 247
The Unchangeable..............................247

CHAPTER THIRTY-THREE
Charity: Live with Love and Equity • 251
Charity is the Equalizer of Injustice and Inequity 254
Give without Desire of Return..................255
The Joy of Giving.............................256

CHAPTER THIRTY-FOUR
Desire: The Heart's Desire is the Source of Creation • 259
The Image and Likeness of a Creator 261
The Innate Flame..............................262
Blueprint of Creativity: The Source 263

The OM Vibration 264
A Spiritual Polarity of Light and Dark 266

CHAPTER THIRTY-FIVE
Faith: Trust Your Creative Birthright ♦ 271
The Door of Symbols. 272
Faith is "Knowing" 274

CHAPTER THIRTY-SIX
Stillness: The Law of Alignment ♦ 277
Stillness Gathers and Aligns Energies 279
The Revitalizing Breath 280
Silence is Golden 281
Step Out of Self 282

CHAPTER THIRTY-SEVEN
Creation: The Law of ONE ♦ 285
The Restoration of Earth 287
Stand as a Co-Creator 288
The Cycle of ONE 291

CHAPTER THIRTY-EIGHT
Creativity: The Law of Oneness ♦ 295
Creativity is the "Becoming". 299
Creation is ONE - Creativity is Part of 300
The Liturgy of Co-creation. 301

CHAPTER THIRTY-NINE
Creative Change ♦ 305

Canada and the New Humanity....................306
The Perfection Within 306
Lake Louise...................................308
Global Warming................................309
A Golden City Dedicated to the Violet Flame 310
Greenland....................................311
Choices Create Abundance........................312
"Take My Hand" 314
Golden City of Brotherhood.......................316
The Coast Mountains 317

CHAPTER FORTY
Abundant Seas ♦ 319

New Sealife...................................320
Northwest Territories..........................320
Pole Shift and the Gulf of Alaska....................321
The Canadian West Coast........................321
The Yukon 323
Global Warming and New Transportation Routes 324
Calgary and Edmonton.........................325
Saskatchewen: North America's New
   Bread Basket 327

CHAPTER FORTY-ONE
Sweet Smile ♦ 329

The Aquifers of Manitoba........................330
Ottawa, a Center for Art........................332

CHAPTER FORTY-TWO
Perfection of the Flame ♦ 333

Map of Canada 334
Water and Magnetic Attraction 335
Ontario: A New Culture of Beauty. 339
Hudson Bay and James Bay .341
The Great Lakes: Unity Lake .343
Baffin Island and the Final Pole Shift. 344
The Canadian East Coast. 346
Saint Lawrence River and Seaway 347
Mini Ice Age 347
Perfection of the Spiritual Flame 348
Toronto and Lake Ontario 349

SPIRITUAL LINEAGE OF THE VIOLET FLAME	351
GLOSSARY	353
INDEX	369
ABOUT LORI TOYE	383
ABOUT I AM AMERICA	386

Foreword

Out of this world's chaos, there really is a way forward with Love, Wisdom, and Power. Our Higher Selves await our recognition and our surrender to who we really are. Who to better guide us than those who have gone before us, who have mastered the Earth energies and ascended? These Masters are not only reachable, but by focusing on any one of them, their revitalizing energies return to us. They stand beside us, in service to our growth and Self-actualization.

There is, of course, Jesus, also known as Sananda; Saint Germain, who lived as Joseph; El Morya, who lived as King Arthur; and Kuthumi, who lived as Saint Francis of Assisi. These last two were also two of the biblical Wisemen and are still following the bright Star of the Way Shower. There are so many more but these four appeared to Lori Toye and she, in turn, brings them to us. They carry the Divine Plan to restore the Earth to her pristine condition and bring every man, woman, and child Home.

This is a sacred text. It emanates the timeless, universal constants of Love and Light and can guide the course of humankind into a Golden Age. As these great Masters come forward to share the Wisdom of the Ages, they light a path that we can follow. They bring us Twelve Jurisdictions, or universal laws, which are so alive and transformative, that we need only follow their sequence to become Co-creators. They show us how to align our wills, which brings forth Harmony. Harmony, in turn, brings us Abundance, and builds further through the sequence of Clarity, Love, Service, Illumination,

Cooperation, and Charity. Then, we learn that our Desire links us to the Creator. Our Faith holds that Desire as it enters the Stillness, which is ever-giving, and then manifests as an act of Creation.

When Lori was visited by these Masters, it shocked her out of a conventional life into a quest for the discipline and skills necessary to bring forth their Teachings. Her devotion and hard work has put these Teachings into our hands. May this Love from the Masters enliven our hearts and lift us into the Light of the Mother/Father God that Never Fails.

> Om Eandra (A special blessing for the Earth Mother),
> *Elaine Cardall*

Preface

When I first heard the term, "Earth Changes," in the late eighties, I was preparing for a slide presentation of the *I AM America Map*. My eyes darted over a small flyer for the event: "The Earth Changes Prophecies of Sun Bear" in bold. We had been asked to present the *I AM America Map* at the Gardenia Center in Sandpoint, Idaho. And we would be sharing the stage with a member of the Bear Tribe, a Native American medicine group who was then centered near Spokane, Washington.

"Earth Changes" was terminology coined by the Association for Research and Enlightenment (ARE) to describe the sleeping prophet Edgar Cayce's apocalyptic visions of the future. In the eighties most of us had no idea what this really meant. Other than this flyer, the most that I knew about Earth Changes was the related field of "psychic archaeology," based on the research of geologist Jeffrey Goodman. I remember that I was standing in the living room of my small home on Eighth Street in Lewiston, Idaho, when I first saw his "Earth Changes Map." It was a small black and white drawing of the United States inside a paperback written by Goodman that was published in the late seventies: "We are the Earthquake Generation." I glanced at it and then asked my partner to close the book. Eerily, this map looked similar to the sketches of the *I AM America Map* that we had been working with during our trance sessions. I was afraid that seeing Goodman's information might influence my work.

When I finished the trance work on this project, there were more than eighty recorded sessions. However, by the time that the Map was published in 1989, we had only transcribed the information regarding the changes—about one-fifth of the information that we had audiotaped. The bulk of the remaining material was personal guidance and spiritual teachings, alongside descriptions of spiritual techniques and how to use them.

My partner was fascinated with Earth Changes. Since he had studied the Edgar Cayce prophecies, which had been received as far back as 1934, he was eager to learn updated information. And he, like so many novices to this type of material, was obsessed with time frames. This was the topic of many questions he directed to the Spiritual Teachers and they often circumvented a direct answer by replying with spiritual parables and innuendo. This really frustrated him. Finally they answered with a telepathic message that I relayed: "They are indicating that the first events begin in 1992 and end in 2000 (A.D.)." Yet several days later the Spiritual Teachers gently reminded us that dates are indeed only "reference points," and they reiterated to *not publish* or to openly share dates. For whatever reason, my partner forgot or ignored this guidance and became certain that the prophesied changes would literally begin in the year 1992. Ironically, the session on "reference points" was never included in our published material and it was only transcribed years after the *I AM America Map* was published. Since publication was already complete, this critical addendum was forgotten and was filed away for more than twenty years in a large vinyl binder that we referred to as the "Blue Book."

When I reviewed transcripts from this decades-old file for possible inclusion in the book *A Teacher Appears*, I stumbled across the statement about reference points. It goes like this:

Question: "Are you ready to work on the Map?"

Saint Germain responds telepathically, "*Always trust. Remember I AM the Way, I AM the Truth . . .*" I repeat this aloud to Dan.

Response: "Is there any of this information that we should not give out?"

Again, I repeat their telepathic response: "*Definitely the dates.*"

Response: "Okay."

Saint Germain again reiterates: "*Dates are only reference points.*"

My curiosity was piqued . . . what exactly is a reference point? I searched the term to learn that a reference point is a "position in the landscape of time, where one can evaluate or weigh probability." Such a point is placed so we can initiate comparison between actual events, prophesied events, and the possibility of their timing.

I eagerly shared this information with a business associate when he reminded me, "You know, there is a date on the *I AM America Map* . . . I believe it is year 2000. I think that influences your credibility." Then he suggested that we change the copy on the *I AM America Map*.

This published text is what Dan had written many years ago. For some reason, even though Saint Germain had emphasized that we not rely on dates to interpret the material, Dan couldn't seem to think any other way. At first glance, most people tend to view this type of information with this conventional perspective. By its nature, a prediction is ripe with risk, chance, and probability. Yet most of us view predictions are inordinately literal, right or wrong. I, too, originally shared this viewpoint. But after several years of working with and deepening my own spiritual experience through the teachings, my understanding of the *I AM America Map* expanded and I began to appreciate just *why* the Spiritual Teachers shied away from timelines.

By the mid-nineties, we rewrote the Map's copy and planned to publish the change, but unfortunately this never happened. This was a time when many other prophesying Earth Changes mapmakers were climbing aboard the millennial band wagon, and some were changing and covering up their past, inaccurate predictions. We decided to remain transparent about the I AM America message. After all, the Map was not prediction—it was prophecy.

If you have read or explored any of the I AM America teachings, you may already know that prophecy *is not* prediction. In fact, the Spiritual Teachers' stance is that prophecy is a timely warning, imparted to help one to avert, ameliorate, or to altogether avoid possible calamity. And more importantly, most prophecies are accompanied by vital solutions that help to transform outcomes. This philosophic notion is explored throughout the I AM America Teachings and explained in-depth in my book *The Ever Present Now*. Prophecy's rich metaphor is designed to engender healing at many levels. And the Spiritual Teachers place an important emphasis on states of human consciousness and our ability to change current situations and create new realities.

PREFACE

While the information you're about to read was first published more than twenty years ago as the *New World Atlas Series*, I can truthfully state that it hasn't been until the last few years that I have had the maturity and insight to be able to grasp and fully understand this material in order to extract its subtle message.

Prophetic works often reveal dichotomy: they are both metaphoric and literal. Please reread, meditate upon, and carefully contemplate the information in this book. Over time I have discovered that these transcripts are vital "living texts." That is, your evolving consciousness is an important factor in your comprehension of something that is as alive as you are; as your comprehension changes, so will the text. As you immerse yourself in reading, certain phrases may jump out at you that are intimately intended for that moment. Or, you may begin to have spiritual experiences that in some appropriate way mirror the meaning of a spiritual lesson.

Through the process of revisiting the prophecies and teachings for this series, my structural editor and I delved deeply into the I AM America transcript archive, with the mindful awareness that some transcripts can be easily forgotten and that their inclusion adds significance to both meaning and interpretation. Originally the *I AM America Map* and *Freedom Star Map* were featured in the *New World Atlas Series*, depicted in excerpts and drawings. We concluded that since this information was so much more than Earth Changes and contained vital spiritual wisdom for the New Times, the emphasis should be changed. So we removed the Maps, and if you'd like to view them you can peruse the complete collection in the latest full-color edition of the *I AM America Atlas* or purchase them individually from our bookstore.

With this in mind, the word "Atlas" no longer seemed an accurate fit for this series, so we chose *New World Wisdom*. Interestingly, some etymologists suggest that the word "wisdom" is the *way of knowing* . . . not the *known*. Lao Tzu says, "The wise man is one who knows what he does not know." *New World Wisdom Series* is about our journey into the spiritual darkness of the unknown to discover and redeem our essential inner light.

The teachings in this book contain information that explains how human consciousness has the ability to change and transform, and how this microcosmic effect literally extends to guiding social and cultural values, and onward to physically reshape the planet's weather, sensitive ecosystems, and geography. This unique co-creation is based on the restructuring of our spiritual virtue and innate goodness by a conscious cultivation of the *Twelve Jurisdictions*, shared by the Spiritual Teachers. This new way of thinking allows our emergent consciousness to embrace the ONE through engaging our own personal Ascension process. The Spiritual Teachers call this process the "BE-Coming." This development engenders the growth of a new global, cultural consciousness—the Golden Age.

I express heartfelt appreciation to Dan, whose personal quest into the spiritual realms sparked my entrance into trance work and the genesis of this work. He is the monitor for chapters one through twenty-three. Thanks and gratitude to my husband, Lenard Toye who serves as monitor throughout the rest of this book. He also channels the Jurisdictions of Service, Cooperation (masculine version), Charity, Stillness, and Creativity. His years of loving service and his contribution to this work are invaluable and truly cherished.

PREFACE

I acknowledge the editors who helped to sculpt this manuscript for publishing: Dorothy Malville, Elaine Cardall, and Betsy Robinson. And a nod of grateful recognition to Athena, who donated the funds for its first printing as *New World Atlas*. No doubt, even this book would have never been printed without her help and generosity many years ago.

Above all, eternal thanks to the *Dear ones*, the Spiritual Teachers who carefully guided and crafted the spiritual wisdom of this book. I treasure their constant and profound presence, and the gift of their unfathomable, precious, and unending love.

~ Lori Toye

About the I AM America Maps

Since the *New World Wisdom Series* centers on the prophecies and spiritual teachings of both the *I AM America Map* and *Freedom Star World Map*, I would be remiss not to share some interesting stories about both Maps. Through the years we have listened to hundreds of stories of people's reaction to the Maps.

First, I think it is important for you to understand that we consider the Maps sacred objects. That is, they hold and contain a spiritual vibration that many notice, especially when they first view or touch them.

Because of this we almost never fold a Map. Of course there are exceptions to this, but we try to keep them rolled to resemble as closely as possible the scrolls that the Spiritual Teachers carried from the spiritual ethers and unrolled for us in the trance sessions.

Also, before any *I AM America Map* leaves our office we personally whisper a prayer into it as it is packaged. We've quietly done this for years, and the main reason for this is that when the first *I AM America Maps* were printed the Spiritual Teachers claimed that the sight of a Map could inspire and initiate Spiritual Awakening. Hopefully this prayer assists and protects this heavenly intent as the Map travels through the mail service and arrives at someone's doorstep.

Sacred objects are known to produce otherworldly qualities—spiritual phenomena—and through the years purchasers of our

Maps have telephoned to comment on the "light" that they notice the Maps emit. Or they may detect an unusual scent or perfume. Most report an unusual spiritual feeling like they've seen the Maps before, either in a dream or vision. No doubt the Maps' visual provokes a "knowing."

Now, for the stories.

This first story comes from a woman who spoke at length about the spiritual experiences surrounding her Map. After she hung it up above her home altar she noticed a fragrant smell, almost an ethereal perfume that she could not describe. Several days later she noticed that the Map itself was weeping an oil and when she collected this unusual essence, she discovered that is was indeed the source of the ephemeral scent. As she spoke to Len she enthusiastically commented that she felt that, "The Map was a sacred relic," and that its presence was "assisting her spiritual development and blessed all who came in contact." As far as we know, the Map hung on her wall for several years and continued to weep the scented oil. For whatever reason, this experience was uniquely intended for her to assist her spiritual development.

Another account involves the eastern Indian adept and spiritual teacher, Mother Karunamayi. Considered an incarnation of Divine Mother, Mother Karunamayi travels extensively throughout the world and conveys her inspirational teachings on love, service, meditation, and self-realization. A friend of ours recently gave copies of the *I AM America Maps* to her. She stared at them intently and then asked, "Son, where did you get these Maps?" He answered her question by sharing the unique provenance of the Ascended Masters. She smiled and commented about the Golden Cities: "This information is normally reserved only for the Divine Beings." She was delighted that the Golden City information was now available for the public. I'd like to add that Mother Karunamayi has two ashrams located in Golden Cities: one is located in the Indian *Golden City of Prana*, and the other in the *Golden City of Wahanee*. She is also considering a meditation retreat to be located in the *Golden City of Gobean*. These locations are cited on the *Freedom Star World Map*.

About fifteen years ago a gentle spirit contacted the I AM America office. The man explained a series of detailed Earth Changes dreams that the abbot of his monastery had recently experienced, and the community questioned if it was time to leave the San Francisco area. The only problem was that since he was a Buddhist monk he had few resources. Len explained that if he could pay for the postage, we would gladly send him our Maps free of charge. The gentleman wrote about a year later to let us know that the entire monastery had moved to Santa Fe, and he thanked us again for the Maps. This is just one of many stories like this.

I've saved the most interesting account for last. I first met Donna in 2010. We were both attending an intimate 2012 gathering where she described her most unique experience: "I was in Mount Shasta for a few days, and dropped into a bookstore." She perused several rows of books when she noticed an unusual Map hanging on the wall with gold letters that read, "I AM America," at the top. She studied the Map for several minutes and knew that she had to purchase it. After she inquired about it, a kind man at the register told her, "Sorry, it's not for sale." Then he added, "But you will receive a copy soon." A bit disappointed, she left the store and returned to her car. She had driven about two miles when she decided that she had to return to the store and ask just one more time if he'd sell her the Map—she had to have it! When she returned to the store location, she couldn't find it. She walked around the block several times and even asked several other store owners, "Do you know where the bookstore is?" They responded with blank looks. Apparently, the store did not exist—was she delusional? It was then that she realized that she had entered an ethereal bookstore and that she had likely seen a glimpse of the future. Donna then remembered the clerk's prophetic words, "You will receive a copy." The year was 1986. The first *I AM America Map* was printed three years later in 1989!

She reached for my hand and held it tightly as tears filled her eyes, "I always knew that someday I would meet you and I would tell you this story."

I asked her, "Well, does my *I AM America Map* match the one you saw?" She quickly replied, "Almost one hundred percent. The only difference is that much of the printing was in gold lettering." And then she added with a smile, "And I knew as soon as I unrolled your *I AM America Map* that this was the map I saw . . . it had the same energy as the one that was hanging on that bookstore's wall."

If you read the book *A Teacher Appears*, you will learn how I sold my house to fund the first press run of the *I AM America Map*. I'd like to reiterate that when I sold my house in the late eighties that *it sold in only twenty-four hours*. Clearly, there was an energy that was guiding and protecting the timely release of this information.

When we faced funding issues with the other Maps, numerous donations generously financed the production and press expenses. For years, the names of these donors were printed on the back of each Map. I am still a bit overwhelmed when I think of their kindness and the sheer faith they placed in this work. Again, I have no doubt that they were touched by the sublime energy of the Spiritual Teachers and their mission for humanity's positive change. The great soul Mahatma Gandhi once said, "Be the change you want to see in the world." The Spiritual Teachers paraphrase this same idea when they remind us, "A Change of Heart can Change the World."

To order an I AM America Map, please go to: iamamerica.com. Or you can write us at P.O. Box 2511, Payson AZ 85547.

CHAPTER ONE

Opening

"When the student is ready, the Master appears."
— BUDDHIST PROVERB

The venerated astrologer KT Boehrer told me in a personal reading that perhaps the most difficult time an astrologer must determine is the ever important starting point of an event. After years of practice as an astrologer myself, I must agree. We most often remember that moment in time when something significant in our life ends. My starting point, however, in Ascended Master teaching was unforgettable. I was a young, twenty-two-year-old advertising sales rep for a small weekly newspaper and I had an appointment with a potential client. She stood at the counter and pointed her finger directly at me as I entered her store and stated with an uncanny certainty, "You have work to do for Master Saint Germain!"

Her compelling words echoed throughout the little shop. "Who is Saint Germain?" I asked. The shop owner motioned to me, and through the tiers of neatly rowed vitamins of the health food store I followed her to a back office, where she pointed to a large framed portrait on the wall. The words *Comte de Saint Germain* were carefully scripted in gold letters on the painting. As I viewed the image I noted young aristocratic features and he looked about thirty years old. The portrait was dated around the late eighteenth century, yet oddly I recognized his face. I had known Saint Germain before.

This unusual meeting instigated a spiritual awakening that introduced me to some of the most exceptional and inspirational information I had ever encountered. Since I was raised in the conventional customs of the conservative Missouri Synod Lutheran Church, I had never heard of subjects like meditation, spiritual development, or reincarnation. The owner of the shop—Florence—became my first teacher of the Ascended Master tradition.

By 1983 my passage into spiritual knowledge significantly deepened. I became familiar with Ascended Master teachings and insatiably read a variety of works: Baird Spalding's inspirational *Life and Teachings of the Masters of the Far East*; the captivating and devotional *I AM Discourses* written by Guy and Edna Ballard under the direction of Saint Germain; and various metaphysical and Ascended Master authored teachings. I began the wondrous and longed-for journey to connect with my Higher Self and the God within—the I AM.

OPENING

THE APPEARANCE OF SAINT GERMAIN

Nineteen eighty-three was also the year my second daughter was born. My initiation into higher consciousness was steadily grounded by caring for a newborn and two rambunctious pre-schoolers, hanging laundry, cooking meals, hoeing weeds, and tending gardens. Through the polarities of lofty possibility and the constant demands of young motherhood, I discovered a secret sanctuary in the profound and indelible teachings of the Great White (Light) Brotherhood. This year also marked the beginning of many personal changes. I would wake at night and hear an audible voice call my name. In the darkness of the room I felt a presence. On one occasion an ethereal form materialized at the foot of my bed and I realized it was Saint Germain. My hand reached to touch him and he vanished. There were no special messages or insightful words of wisdom; just his presence, a timeless presence.

I would often recall the radiance of this remarkable presence upon my nightly surrender to sleep; I prayed and asked the Brotherhood to contact me.

FOUR WHITE-ROBED BEINGS UNROLL A MAP

For several months nothing happened, just ordinary, peaceful sleep. Then it happened: an experience not like a dream. An experience often communicated by shamans and prophets as a vision.

In the early-morning hours of sleep I was aware I had left my body. I entered a room resembling a schoolroom. This room held a large desk, and four beings clad in white robes were present. The beings gently guided my attention to a rolled manuscript placed upon the desk. As they unrolled the document, it was an obvious map of the United States; yet, this map was noticeably different. The map illustrated major changes of land and water. It displayed new rivers, canyons, and coastlines. Light and radiance exuded from the map and I sensed its content, alive with conscious knowledge. More importantly, the map revealed significant geologic changes when compared to our present-day Earth. Clearly, this map was a message.

This vision repeated over a four-month period. Each vision was similar: I entered a room where I was greeted by the presence of four white-robed beings—Master Teachers—alongside the map of major Earth Change.

I shared the vision with a friend. She commented, "The Earth Changes have been prophesied for a long time, and we are now entering that period of time. After the changes, many predict we will enter a Golden Age."

"Just another unexplained dream . . . ," I reasoned. Nothing to act on. And there was little I could do anyway as my life was filled with the routines of children and housework. The vision stopped; yet, within I sensed something different. A small seed had been planted.

Five years later, faced with the stress of a painful divorce and rebuilding my life as a single mother, I attended spiritual meditation classes. I again shared the vision with another friend, a student of the acclaimed Edgar Cayce material. Captivated, he hoped we could re-create the map's detail and obtain more clarity regarding its message. The idea intrigued me too.

We agreed to meet and work in the early morning—four a.m. The mornings were quiet and during these peaceful hours my consciousness seemed receptive to a meditative state. The first sessions were difficult, the work was slow, and the information sparse. I recalled a previous teaching from Saint Germain about how one may raise one's consciousness to the level of a Master Teacher's. He instructed, "First, you must *feel*." In my mind I evoked the image and the radiant energy of the Master as he had appeared to me. The next step was sensing this subtle energy, and applying the *feeling as force*—better known as *energy vibration*—to consciously journey to a higher state of awareness. It is my perception that as I raised my energy to enter this plane, the Ascended Masters simultaneously lowered their vibration to meet me. After several attempts the method worked, and I successfully re-entered the room of the vision. The four white-robed beings introduced themselves as Saint Germain, El Morya, Kuthumi, and Sananda. The seed had sprouted.

As our ability to work together developed and grew, many other Ascended Beings were introduced and gave input to the map and its many supplementary teachings. Looking back, it is now apparent this information was given in a wholly structured, yet divinely disordered manner! I would later learn the Ascended Master phrase to better explain this phenomenon: "there are no mistakes, ever, ever, ever!"

ASCENDED MASTERS AND THE CHRIST CONSCIOUSNESS

The Great White Brotherhood is best described as a cooperative group of souls, through the masterful use of energy, have individually attained a state of spiritual liberation and no longer require a physical body, since they are freed from the Wheel of Karma. Ascended Masters employ the Christ Consciousness, and their activites mirror Universal Laws and Universal Principles. Apparently their organization functions beyond the scope of our everyday human limitations, and members comprise literally millions. Many Masters are associated with different planets and solar systems. Their interaction with the Earth regarding the prophesied Earth Changes, or *transition* as they often describe this important time, is solely based upon their vows of *service to humanity*. This important mentoring is ultimately designed to enlighten and usher humanity into a New Age of expanded awareness, conscious thinking, living, and *Be-ing*. It is also my belief that the Earth Changes information was given with a great deal of love for humanity and was never intended to instill fear. The Masters have offered their sacred knowledge to warn us, and also to prepare us. This information is an urgent plea intended to instigate a collective healing process for ourselves and our planet—physically, emotionally, and spiritually.

As you read, you will note the beginning chapters of this first volume of teachings include most of the information surrounding the Ascended Masters' Earth Changes Map—the *I AM America Map*. Each chapter comprises a series of channeled sessions and reviews the map in the presence of the Master Teachers. As my ability to channel developed and matured, so did the information. So please be patient with the choppy and sometimes obtuse wording of the trance-channeled sessions. You'll see as the teaching progresses, so does the fluidity of the text. Perhaps some of the most fascinating teachings in this book are the Ascended Masters' *Twelve Jurisdictions*, a series of spiritual lessons which are key to understanding the universal laws underlying the prophesied New Consciousness on Earth. The Master Teachers specifically asked for these spiritual teachings to accompany the prophetic Earth Change material.

I AM thankful to be of Service to the Ascended Masters. Their radiance has blessed me with an abundance of friends, experiences, purpose, and love. I offer their wonderful teachings with the hope that indeed a personal change in your consciousness may change the outcome of prophesied events.

Truly, a change of heart can change the world.

What is critical is that we try.

CHAPTER TWO

Beginning Notes

*"A journey of a thousand miles must
begin with a single step."*
- LAO TSU

The beginning sessions were tedious, and the information was given in a very general manner. From the first tape, my friend comments: "The other night when she (Lori) was in this trance state I started quizzing her, asking her questions and she was able to get the answers very easily. She can evidently look at the map and see the overall perspective and sees herself drawing the new coastline on this map. When asked to see something at a closer perspective, say our region here, she is able to go down into the map, like a view from a cloud or satellite and see the details of the coastline. So we've purchased some maps and we are starting with an overall large perspective of the whole coastline of the country.

From what she has shared so far, these beings show probably 80% of the state of Maine being lost. Very little changes in the southern states on the coast and the Carolinas. They have shown her a fault line going down through the New

York, Washington D.C. area and about half of those states right along the coastline breaking up. They have shown the Mississippi basin, the Missouri River dropping to a point where an arm of the Gulf of Mexico will sweep clear up almost to the Montana, Canadian border. Much of the Western States drop off, from Seattle down to the Wyoming area. The whole inland Columbia Basin plateau sinks, pretty much following the Columbia River."

GENESIS OF THE GOLDEN CITIES

"In the last session she saw three pins, diamond headed pins. One was close to the Puffer Butte area over in Washington, right on the breaks of the Grande Ronde, another pin was up close to Steptoe, if not on the Steptoe Butte, and the third pin was over on the Idaho-Montana Border line. She was told that the area within this triangle was a spiritually protected area. It would be protected from most of the Earth Changes or devastations because it was a gateway and would remain clear for transportation and communication.

At one point, the Masters took her pencil and handed her a golden pen and started pointing and telling her the new names of some of the points on the map. Then she took the gold pen and drew the names in."

It was apparent at this time that this map of Earth Changes contained more than just geophysical changes, that there would be detailed information on what we now understand as Vortex areas.

My perception of these areas is that they are locations where Golden Cities would precipitate, Vortex areas where the Masters will reside, healing, teaching and helping the masses of people re-establish their beliefs and civilizations in the East and in the West."

Our excitement and commitment to this project grew as the Masters continued to give more information. The specific details amazed us. We realized the need to record these details, so we purchased a small hand-held tape recorder and started to record each session.

CHAPTER THREE
with Saint Germain

Golden Crystal Age

"The minutes and the seconds tick,
and the awakening is at hand."
- SANANDA

ASCENSION VALLEY

There's a hand holding a pen, and I must write. I've got two letters, and they are to be written on the Vortex area in our region, "A, S," and then "C," spelling out "Ascension Valley." They have more names for us for the map.

Question: "Is this the valley which runs north and south?"

There will be a valley. It's going to be very large and beautiful. It's location is not in the central Idaho area, but more into Northern Idaho. It is near the town of St. Maries, and close to where Lake Coeur d'Alene will drain; in fact much of the lake will drain into this valley. After these changes the climate will be tropical. There are mountain ranges on both sides of this valley and there will be very little wind there.

THE CASCADE MOUNTAINS

Question: "What other changes are they showing you on the map?"

   I'm starting at Vancouver and traveling down to Seattle . . . Seattle is gone. Mt. Baker is an island, and so is Mt. Rainier. In fact, the whole Cascade range will become islands. The town of Ellensburg is gone, covered by water. The state of Washington is covered by ocean waters.

[Editor's Note: After receiving detailed information of this nature we would periodically stop, and pen in the coastline as the Masters revealed it.]

Question: "Is Saint Germain with you?"

   Yes, and he is speaking about the Golden Age in reference to the Golden Cities. He says, this age will be referred to as a Golden Crystal Age, and that these gateways, or Vortex areas, are protected areas for interaction with spiritual energy.

Question: "Continue on down the coastline. What are they showing you?"

   The coastline continues all the way down to La Grande, Oregon, and the Wallowa Mountains become a beautiful chain of islands. They erode very slowly, first at the end of a peninsula and eventually into islands. The coastline goes to La Grande and then it comes back west over into the Baker area and central Oregon. It curves back around almost to the California border and then it starts jogging back east again. This peninsula I'm speaking about extends almost to Crater Lake. Then it curves back, going clear up to the California border, and then it slips back down and goes to Utah, through the northern part.

Question: "I wonder how Idaho will become a coastline?"

There is a lot of seeping water, and a back flow of this water into the Snake River Canyon. Then the whole land mass begins to slip into a very massive sinking. It's important that we draw this information.

MOUNT SHASTA

That night I had another vision. I saw that the peninsula going down into the tip of California includes Mount Shasta. The Masters presented a series of maps, in a series of overlays showing that during the times of Earth Changes there would be a peninsula of land including Mount Shasta, and that it would eventually erode away and dissolve into a long island chain. They renamed these newly formed islands the Emerald Islands. The Masters assured me in this vision that a small portion of every state would be left; all the 50 states, even though it might be a small portion.

They gave more information on the Vortex areas, and that the golden pins determined their locations. These Vortex areas had a definite shape, resembling a pyramid. The Vortex areas serve as great nerve endings during the Time of Changes, as a focus for great spiritual energy.

CHAPTER FOUR
with Saint Germain

Meteorites

"These stars, count them to become your companions, your watchers, and your keepers."
- PETER THE EVERLASTING

OREGON

Question: "An earthquake alone cannot cause the massive changes you are showing. What else occurs?"

They are showing me that Central Oregon will sink as a result of an earthquake, but preceding this is a massive shower of meteorites, sending a terrific ash cloud into the atmosphere. This ash cloud causes tremendous rains to fall, and the increased pressure on the planet from this continuous flow of rain, causes slippage of fault lines and massive earthquakes. After the changes the skies will open and the rains will stop.

Question: "The skies will open, do they mean the manifestation of the Golden Cities or that the rain will stop?"

Yes, the cities, then it will stop. The cleansing is given by the four elements: fire, water, earth, and the wind. The wind isn't going to hit this area, but it will hit the East Coast. The biggest fear in our area will be from fire and the ash fallout. Also there will not be any sun for two years. Many people will try to heat their homes using wood, but there will be restrictions because of the extra smoke it puts into the air which will be very polluted. It is important that we look into alternative energy sources now.

CHAPTER FIVE
with Saint Germain

Golden Cities

"From this day, the Light of the Golden Sun will be greatly intensified into the Heart of Terra."
- APOLLO

On top of the map is a sheet of paper. They're writing across it Abundance, Prosperity, and Healing and stressing the importance of these words. These words are to be directly associated with the new bay that forms in the Pacific Northwest.

GOLDEN CITIES OF THE WESTERN UNITED STATES

There's a second set of words ... Transformation, Harmony, Peace, more words associated with the bay that forms around Utah, Arizona, and Colorado. And now they are showing that a second Vortex will be formed. There are three more pins. One is in Mesa, the lower pin. The size or configuration of this Vortex is exactly the same as the Vortex in the Northwest.

Question: "So the one at Mesa would be in the same position as the one in our area?"

There will be another Golden City at the apex.

Question: "Does it have a name?"

It starts with G, and now they are writing the other letters, G O B E A N. Gobean. The Vortex in the Northwest has a name, too, S H A L A H A H. Shalahah. They are showing me a gold star on what is now the Mexican and California border. They say this marks the location of an important mineral deposit.

Question: "Can you tell what the mineral is?"

It's gold ore, mixed with a black kind of substance. Now they are placing gold stars all over the map. There is more information regarding the Vortices. They overlap mathematically and geometrically.

Question: "Do they have more Earth Change information for us?"

MISSISSIPPI RIVER

The Mississippi River will almost cut the nation in two. It's much narrower at the top and widens quite a bit at the bottom. It's very wide down at the bottom and covers and takes a large part of Texas away, with Islands in the mouth of it.

Question: "Do you see the Great Lakes draining into it?"

The bottom lake drains near Chicago. There is another Vortex by the Denver area. The location of the apex of the Gobean Vortex is between Mesa and Albuquerque. Denver is one of the western points to another central Vortex.

There is a channel from the Bay of Harmony that goes right to the mountains of Denver. It will be a passage from the East to another apex up over the mountains to Denver, also a passage to the other river. This is a wide, fresh water river, and they are naming it The River of Cooperation because of the immense amount of cooperation which will occur between this river and the people living near it. Eventually, this becomes a source for irrigation, and the area surrounding it will become a strong agricultural area for the nation.

They are also showing that the lands in Eastern Montana and in the Dakotas are pretty much undisturbed.

CONTINENTAL DIVIDE

Question: "Do you see any more changes?"

A new Continental Divide. A new mountain range will form. It starts in Central Canada, and follows the flow of the River of Cooperation. It forms between what we know now as the Mississippi River and the Rocky Mountains, and extends down almost to New Mexico. In between the Rockies and the new divide a beautiful grassland is formed. It's beautiful. Close to where Denver is now.

Question: "Is this mountain chain close to the Mississippi River?"

The River of Cooperation follows the present channel of the Mississippi, only it is much wider. This new mountain chain is more into the Kansas area, and then continues to the upper Eastern corner of New Mexico. The Vortex on the East side of Denver is to provide a gateway through that mountain chain over that divide, from the Rockies to the new mountains.

Question: "Will the present Rockies by Denver sink some or will the new mountains just be that much taller?"

They will shift a little. It's more erosive than anything. But that erosion will take longer, into a period of time after the major changes, so will the new mountain range.

Question: "So that mountain range will not be there by year 2000 then?"

These changes continue and they are gradual. This new mountain range will be formed in the Golden Age, they aren't giving a date for its formation, but it will begin to form at the onset of the Golden Age and serve as a symbol to a great age. The new bay surrounding the Denver area will be formed before this age.

Question: "What do you see the rest of the coastline looking like towards Florida?"

There is a small part of Florida not there, and a portion of Maine that's gone. They are placing a pyramid on the map in the ocean waters near Florida, off the East Coast. At the top of this pyramid is a gold capstone.

CHAPTER SIX
with Saint Germain

Structure

"This is an Age of Cooperation."
- SAINT GERMAIN

THE MOUNTAIN OF LIGHT

During a channeling session, I see a mountain in the Ascension Valley with a beam of light coming out of it.

Question: "Is this mountain right down in the valley or is it along the edge?"

It looks like it's more along the edge but you can look right off the other side of the mountain and see a deep canyon. You can see all the colors in the canyon and there are trees too. You can hike up to the top of this mountain, and there I'm seeing massive Ascensions taking place. Many people will know about this mountain, but won't travel to it until they are ready.

Question: "Do you see a name for the mountain?"

The name has a K and a M in it. There's no given name. Some people call it the Mountain of Light. Other people call it Ascension Mountain. The scenery surrounding this area is spectacular when you stand up on top of the mountain and look down. There are a lot of shades and hues of pink. It's absolutely gorgeous!

Question: "Will the large Vortex area still be there (in the Northwest) after the Times of Changes and will it still be needed?"

Oh yes, it will still be there. They are saying that this is a fundamental structure.

Question: "What about the city at the apex of the Vortex?"

You can see it, but there is a very thin layer, like a sheet of Mica or something, between it and the Earth.

Question: "Is this during the Times of Changes or current?"

The cities are in existence now, but after the Times of Changes they become much more apparent. I can see some of the architecture of this city. They call it a Golden City. I'm seeing a series of buildings; they're all faced in gold and they have an interesting structure, similar to a pyramid, but not exactly a pyramid.

Question: "What else do you see on the map?"

You've drawn the River of Cooperation too wide. They say the measurements are 2.82 KM, and it flows into a salt water bay in Louisiana, which is mostly an island. It's very erosive. The bottom coastline of Florida will be at an angle.

WASHINGTON D.C.

Question: "What about Washington D.C. and the Philadelphia area?"

They are showing a huge crystal coming right out of the ocean, on the Atlantic side. This is some sort of power source. However, we won't be allowed to use it for some time. They now show that another one has been planted too, on the North side.

Question: "What does this one mean?"

It contains records of medical procedures; but the use of these records will not be revealed until the Golden Age. There will be a big bay where New York once was.

There will be no islands in this bay, and the wind will blow there for a long time. They are naming it Reconciliation Bay.

Question: "Is there a Vortex in that area?"

There once was. But the energy has been misplaced, so nothing will be allowed there for a long time.

Question: "What about Washington D.C.?"

The symbols of our nation present in this area will be given protection. They are saying that this area has been of great Service to our country, but after the changes, it will not longer be the political center of our country. People who travel to Washington D.C., will travel there only to view the symbols and their historical significance.

Question: "Where will the political center move to?"

They are showing that there will be several political centers in the country.

CHAPTER SEVEN
with Saint Germain

Coastlines

*"The surface of this planet has offered herself to assist
in the cleansing of the lower bodies of mankind."*
- SAINT GERMAIN

WASHINGTON STATE

Comment: "We have the general outline of the map now. Let's try to get the details down as close as we can. Let's just start up by Seattle and go clear around to see if there's anything that needs to be altered."

It changes quite a bit in Washington State. The coastline goes even a little bit up into the British Columbia area, then back down near the Okonagan Valley. The coastline, in the beginning, follows the Columbia River. Eventually the coastline is close to Spokane and Pullman, Washington. The coastline is 18 kilometers from Pullman. There are some small islands. The Cascade range will become islands, and a small portion of Seattle will remain on an island. It comes down like a hook. The Olympic Peninsula is still there, remaining as an island. Vancouver Island is only about half there, the top portion gone. The water rises there approximately 750 feet.

Question: "Is this caused by rising waters or shifting lands?"

MELTING ICE AND THE NEW MAGNETIC NORTH

Water is rising and earth is shifting. Ice is beginning to melt and the ice will shift it. The polar change will cause the equator to move, and the waters will be shifted, higher in places and lower in others. They are showing that the outside points of the energy vortices point to the new magnetic North Pole. The huge island formed by the Cascade Range starts as a peninsula, then the rising waters will erode them into the islands.

Question: "What are the names?"

The Islands of Fortune.

CHAPTER EIGHT
with Saint Germain

Five Stars

*"The Earth Changes will usher in a
new way of thinking and being."*
- SAINT GERMAIN

Saint Germain is saying that by using the configuration of the Maltese Cross, we will understand the mathematics of the energy Vortices. This is very important and we should take note of it. He is also saying never to forget love for yourself and to extend love into this project. He is saying that the love surrounding this project is very important.

Response: "I know, and I appreciate their love and support. Should we work on the map now?"

THE GREAT LAKES

They are showing details of a peninsula around Mount Shasta ... also more details of the drainage of the Great Lakes. The one lower lake is definitely going to drain.

Question: "Do the other lakes remain pretty much the same?"

When the one drains it will change the appearance of the others. They will form one large lake which they are naming Unity Lake. The lower lake drains into the River of Cooperation.

Question: "How far up does the River of Cooperation go?"

It goes almost up into the Dakotas. It follows the present path of the Mississippi, and it's drainage goes into the present Gulf of Mexico. During the worst of the changes, some people will think it will divide the United States, but it won't.

The two other lakes to the Northeast will drain through a river seventy-seven miles to where it meets the other lake. It will be a very wide river.

Question: "What will it's name be?"

It won't exist. It's only purpose is to drain. I see the remaining lakes as all one lake, Unity, one large lake.

Question: "Is there anything else we should be aware of?"

Washington DC will have tremendous winds, very cold winds.

Question: "So the West Coast will be more tropical, but the East Coast will have a more frigid climate?"

They are now holding a candle to the map, close ... to Chicago, Illinois. Now, there's another pin. This is an outer point for another Vortex. It's the northeastern point.

Question: "What was the candle?"

It is a symbol they use to get our close attention.

Question: "Do you see a large population area where Chicago now is?"

There will be a lot of water throughout the town, but it will survive. This will be a great cleansing.

Question: "What about Denver, will it be affected much by the changes physically?"

Not a lot, but it will feel the earthquake tremendously. The inlet from the sea in the Denver area comes in to the present Continental Divide line and crosses or cuts through it to create a new transportation route. There's a weak point, or fault point, where it goes through. This occurs during the height of the most massive changes.

Question: "In your vision the other night, you saw the Earth impacted by a massive meteor, followed by a meteorite shower. Will the Earth Changes be caused by water or the meteor?"

The meteor sets in the weakness. After the meteor hits there will be enough warning in all areas. They say there will be approximately a three month warning.

Question: "What about our monetary system during the Times of Changes?"

During the major earth movements great veins of gold will be opened up in the mountain areas. People will be able to see them. But our monetary system will not be based on gold, and gold will have a different meaning for people.

Question: "What will our new monetary system be based upon? Trade of food, health items, use of a barter system?"

Transportation. People will want to travel to the Golden Cities, and travel to these areas will have a very high value.

Question: "Are there any dates they are willing to share?"

Saint Germain is stating, "Always trust." He is saying, "I AM the way, I AM the truth. Dates are only references."

There is more information regarding the five major Vortices. There is one in the south, and Charleston is the lower east point.

THE FIVE NEW REGIONS OF THE UNITED STATES

Question: "Are there any other Vortices that we have not been shown?"

There are five major ones. There will also be five major regions after the changes, five major political regions. Also, five stars will represent the new nation, still comprised of fifty states. Hawaii will experience changes, but even a portion of it will remain. Alaska will experience some minimal changes.

Question: "Can you see the changes in Alaska?"

The changes will occur in the upper regions. Hawaii will get quite a few tidal waves.

Question: "Will there be lands raising in that area?"

There will be volcanic activity. Hawaii will be changed, because the area will be isolated for some time. This changes the people. They return to a culture that they once knew.

Question: "Do we need to know about a new reference point for the North Pole; will that change?"

Yes it will, and you can line it up with the new Vortices.

He is taking the map, and placing it on the globe. Now he is drawing a circle around the circumference of the globe. The globe is now split from north to south, and you can also split the globe from east to west. He is stating that poles are changing all the time and they will continue to change, and not to worry about pinpoint accuracy regarding this map. He is stating that they are more concerned that we regard the Earth Changes as a way to usher in a new way of thinking and being.

CHAPTER NINE
with Saint Germain

Golden Names

"Send this message to the Earth with love."
- SANANDA

Saint Germain is here to facilitate this information.

Question: "Who else is there?"

There are others here, waiting by the table that the map sits on, and they will help. Kuthumi, Saint Germain, and there is a woman too. I'm not receiving a name; she has blonde hair.

A CULTURAL, GLOBAL CONSCIOUSNESS

Question: "We need the names of the other Golden Cities. What's the one in the Denver area?"

K L E H M A. It's a name of the elders, associated with the American Indian culture.

Question: "Are there more?"

GOBEAN. This is from the Arabic culture, and SHAHALAH is from the Eastern Indian culture. There are also cosmic properties assigned to each city.

Question: "What about the Denver city?"

Continuity and balance. This is to bring a sense of balance to our new country. The area will serve as a central point in America of balance and leadership. It will also serve as a central location for the re-establishment of a monetary system. Klehma is associated with continuity, the balanced transition of the old to the new. There's the candle and they are showing me a gold coin.

Question: "What does it look like?"

It is a blend of the old and the new. On one side is a candle, with the words underneath it, "The Light of God Never Fails." On the other side is an eagle. The coin is dated 2010.

[Editor's Note: We have experienced a slower timing of events and this coin is still to come.]

In the changes, our economy will function on a region to region basis. There won't be a national system until then. There will be the distribution of gold and silver, but in it's older form. Nothing new will be minted. Saint Germain is now giving his thanks to us and appreciation for our willingness to work on this project. He's asking if there is more information he can give.

Question: "What about the Vortex and the Golden City south of the Chicago area, what is it's name?"

The name starts with a M. It seems that is all they are giving at this moment. One attribute assigned to this area is fruition. The other Vortex area in the South is associated with Justice, Liberty, and Freedom.

Question: "What is it's name?"

It is an African name, WAHANEE. They are discussing the fruition Vortex and now are naming it. MALTON. Its name has a Nordic influence, and is associated with Europe.

Question: "Will Lewiston have a different name?"

Yes, Lewisport. It will become a seaport town. They are showing the huge freshwater lake that forms in the Boise Basin area.

Question: "Does it have a name?"

It will be named after the river that forms it, Snake Lake.

CHAPTER TEN
with Saint Germain

Fertile Valley

"This is the Time of Transition."
- SAINT GERMAIN

They've walked through the doors, and Saint Germain says that we have a lot of work to get done today. Do you have questions about the Salt Lake area?

Question: "Yes. The mountains, will they still be there? The mountain range?"

It will be islands for awhile, but then eventually, they too, will be gone. It's very erosive.

Question: "What about the Great Lakes, will the two Eastern lakes drain just like Lake Michigan?"

Yes. They are now naming the islands in the Utah area; the islands will be named the Tablet Islands. The erosion of these islands will be similar to the time frame of the Emerald Islands.

Question: Are there anymore specifics? It sounds like he has more to share? You've seen a pin in the Coeur d'Alene lake.

This is to become a transportation center.

NEW ORLEANS

Question: "So the pass from Coeur d'Alene to Missoula will remain open, also; or will that be in the distant future?"

It is some sort of transportation center, and that's all they say. He's giving me the name now of the bay near New Orleans... the Bay Of Cooperation. In the times to come, this will be reclaimed as a very fertile agricultural area. The area is more like a Delta than a bay, where all the soil collects after tremendous washing and erosion. Eventually, as the waters leave this area, it will become very fertile. It is parallel to an area which once flourished in Egypt. Souls will be embodied here that have once lived in Egypt. They will call it the Fertile Valley.

Question: "How far will the flood go?"

All the way to the bottom of the United States. Many of the low lands will be covered by water. A lot of that bay area is going to fill in with water, but later it will be reclaimed. The channel of the bay ends at the border of the two Dakotas, or near them.

Question: "In constructing this map, should I put in the new Continental Divide or just indicate where it will go?"

It is more important to show the way that the waters will flow. Instead of flowing into Canada, now through the Pacific Northwest, they will flow towards Denver and out that split. There is a big curve toward Denver. They are placing another star on the map, at Bismarck, North Dakota. This is another transportation center.

UNITED STATES: NEW AGRICULTURAL AREAS AND TRANSPORTATION ROUTES

Comment: "Now I understand from Edgar Cayce's work that the big agricultural areas will be in the Albuquerque area and east of there and also into the Dakotas and southern Canada."

They are saying this is correct, but it will take some time for the Albuquerque area to be developed. The North Dakota areas will be the first to be developed.

Question: "And so the major transportation routes of Bismarck, Lewiston, and Coeur d'Alene will be utilized?"

Their gradual build up and economic strength will help the other areas grow. Now in the Maine area they are showing not so much sinking lands, but a combination of water and ice. This creates a lot of pressure in that area. The ice eventually breaks up, and the melting and breaking causes erosion of the land through freezing and thawing. This area will be very unstable, and its climate is unstable. It will be over twenty-five years before there can be a predictable climate in the area. They are also showing the sinking of land around Washington D.C. There will be a shift in one of the lower Great Lakes. As this lake drains, I see the land being depressed, and the depressed area becomes a wide river lake.

Question: "Now, after Lake Michigan has drained, will the flow of Unity Lake be towards the East again?"

No, it will be a self contained lake. It won't drain at all.

WEATHER CHANGES

Question: "Well, I see from New York in the Bay of Reconciliation, straight West, I can see there is the lowest of the two lakes. It's the lower edge of the flood. Is it between those two points?"

I'll ask ... they're drawing arrows on the map, indicating wind. They're showing a wind pattern across to Denver, and then the arrows curve. Once they hit the mountains at Denver, the winds will change.

Question: "Go south?"

It breaks them up and it changes their patterns. From the Maine area, cold winds. And from the Florida area, another wind pattern. There will be a lot of variation, cold winds and warm winds, and these two meet in the center of the states. The winds will meet in extreme contrast. In the Bay of Harmony in the Mesa area, is a desert area that will remain a desert area for some time.

Question: "What are the wind patterns in our area?"

We don't have a lot of wind.

Question: "If we're in a tropical climate, there should be a totally different wind pattern."

They are showing a more self contained climate, and also one in the Mesa area. After the changes, the setting up of the weather crystal device influences the climate. Since the West Coast will be one of the first of the lands to suffer, and will have the most drastic Earth Changes, it will become one of the first to stabilize.

THE UNITED STATES WEST COAST

Question: "Can you see the sinking of Oregon in more detail?"

Again, they are showing a shape with four points. La Grande is one point. Straight across from La Grande is another point. The measurement, straight across to the Willamette Valley, angle it up to the half way distance between La Grande and straight across; bring it back down and you will see your area. They are showing me finer details ... I'll draw it in. The mountains remaining in that area will become islands.

Question: "What else do we need to show on the final outline of the map as far as the coastline and islands go?"

We need to get all the names. Part of the project is showing the higher names. This is for the Golden Crystal Age.

Question: "What about San Diego?"

That will be called the City of Stars. The skies will be very clear over there first, one of the first places where the skies will start to clear.

Question: "But the connection to the mainland there is below sea level now. It would make sense that there would be nothing there."

It will be a peninsula for some time, but eventually it will become islands. They are called the Diamond Islands. Halfway down, into Mexico . . . another bay area.

They are speaking in a language I don't recognize. Saint Germain is saying to rename the islands, the Hawaiian Islands, as the Trinity Islands. Only three islands will still be there that will be inhabitable. Maui is one of them, and the other one starts with an O.

He wants to talk about magnetism and the poles. The shift will occur in the poles 4 degrees, then 12 degrees, then 17. And he says about the Vortices that once you align them, you'll see how each, where they are now, will correspond to those particular numbers. The Vortices are set up on magnetism.

SPIRITUAL PROTECTION

There are the circles. There's a large circle around the Earth itself. It's a golden band. He says it's presence is held at a higher level ... for protection. If this band were not here, these changes would have happened long ago, and the whole continent would sink.

Question: "Does this band correspond with the equator?"

Presently it does, but the equator will be changed. This golden band is something he has sponsored from the Ascended level. Alaska and Hawaii will represent the Oriental cultures. He says it's no mistake that we've saved these states for last to work on, for they are one of the last cultures to be recognized by this new land. Alaska will get warmer. There'll be a lot of surprises as it does get warmer.

Question: "Like mineral deposits?"

A lot of ice will be gone and there will be nothing underneath it. Now they are showing these changes ... towards the northern tip of Alaska. There is a shape like the back of a spoon. The area will melt out. There's basically nothing under it.

There is a change on the Canadian coast. Coming down there will be another bay from Alaska between the states, between Juneau and Vancouver.

Question: "How is the city of Vancouver affected?"

The bay above Vancouver. I'm asking what the purpose is for . . . and they are saying that Canada and the United States will share . . . share in the Earth Changes. This is the meaning of Unity Lake.

The coastline of this Canadian Bay will also serve another purpose. It will make for easier transportation routes to Alaska, where before it has been difficult. They're looking at the map, and he's saying "You did a good job."

Question: "Are there any more additions?"

Over time, Snake Lake will drain, and running out of it will be a coastal river. The Emerald Islands just barely come into the Idaho Border. The Tablet Islands are a little bit bigger . . . and there are two inlets in the Denver area. The two almost form a vee. The vee is not directly centered into Denver. It will form a triangular shape of land, representing the pyramid on the dollar bill. None will live on this vee shape of land . . . it becomes a sacred area.

In the area between Denver and Mesa . . . the beaches are very gradual. The water will not be very deep in places on this coastline . . . the rise of the waters there is a slow, gradual rise. This bay will not become a port area. It will be very hard to navigate in there, almost impossible. There is a reason for this. The water will become very warm, and not very deep at all. It will become a resort area, a place to rest.

There are also small islands that will lead to Gibraltar . . . they will be named the Pathway Islands. These islands will always be there; they are not erosive islands.

Question: "Are there any islands south of Gibraltar?"

No, I don't see any.

Question: "No islands left in the Catalina or Los Angeles area?"

No.

Question: "How does Harvest Bay look?"

There's an incredible amount of energy there. It will become one of the most exciting areas. It will also take a long time for it to be restored. It will seem like the changes will just never end in that area . . . but then the greatest thing could happen there.

Question: "Are there any other major rivers I need to show?"

Cooperation and Opportunity are two . . . Opportunity is the Missouri River and will be navigable up to Bismarck. It becomes wider.

Question: "The way I've sketched in the new Continental Divide, is that approximately right."

It has something to do with Livingston, Montana; it follows the West side of the River of Opportunity and then crosses over the top of it. The river will cross the top of it 128 miles from Livingston. The river will not drain through Denver; there will be smaller rivers draining in that area. The River of Opportunity drains down into the new delta.

Question: "Even the Yellowstone River will continue to drain into the delta then?"

Yes. The new Continental Divide runs with a curve around the Denver Vortex area.

A candle is coming up now. Something we really need to look at. There'll be a very high peak formed.

This peak, mathematically calculates to every Vortex and on the top of it a communication center will be opened. At the top of this mountain is a stream of energy, resembling a silver cord.

This communication center, located on the North side of Denver, West of the Black Hills, will give us all the sense of Oneness. It will send out a wave different from communication that we know now. It is associated with telepathy; telepathy in recognizing the energy of the Higher Self.

CHAPTER ELEVEN
with Saint Germain

Refinement

"Mankind shall feel the resurrection of his true self."
- SAINT GERMAIN

Saint Germain is here, and he is ready to refine the details. He is running his hand up and down the coastline now. We're starting in the delta area.

A little bit of the bay area in that inside delta area is not quite a straight line. There'll be more changes on the West side by Little Rock.

The delta area is wider at the top: five rivers will come in there.

I've asked him if the five rivers correspond to the five Vortices, but he says they don't. The River of Cooperation and the River of Opportunity are great rivers, along with three smaller ones. By the island, Celebration Island, there will be a land appendage that will attach the island to the mainland, but eventually that will erode away.

THE UNITED STATES EAST COAST

There is another bay area up on the Florida coastline . . . it isn't very large, about thirty kilometers in. On the East coastline of Florida almost at the top will be another small bay area, about twenty kilometers in.

The land is going to break up more in a lot of the areas on the East Coast. Where there won't be the major earth movements . . . the land breaks up into islands.

There is breakage in the Norfolk area. There is also a little island in the middle of the Bay of Reconciliation. There is a small inlet in the Philadelphia area, and that coastline is broken up.

The East Coast will be filled with many small islands as the lands break up, and most of the Maine area is under ice. A sheet of ice moves down and covers a portion of the state, extending to the ocean.

A lake forms in the middle of Pennsylvania; it is about half the width of the River of Cooperation.

Question: "What is the name of this lake?"

Some people call it Upper Lake; in the beginning this will be its name.

It's origin is from the Unity Lake drainage. The two eastern Great Lakes drain out towards New York Bay, and into a drainage area associated with Upper Lake.

The Vortex shapes and the angles within the Vortex shape will help you to work out the degrees of the poles. All of the angles there will help you to understand that.

Question: "Are the degree of shifts that he gave us yesterday, degrees from the apex?"

No. But they do correspond to the shape of the energy Vortex. He also says once you get the final pole plotted out, you can take the diamond shape that he gave to you, put it at the top of the pole and you will have a broader-based understanding, a better understanding of all of the shifts.

Question: "But the degree of shift that he gave me yesterday, it can shift four degrees in any of 360 directions. Don't I need some other coordinate there? What's he saying?"

I'm getting twenty-eight.

Do you have more questions?

Question: "No not right now. I'll plot this out, and we'll work more on this in another session. Are there more names to be placed on this map? I have several cities as points of reference for people. What about Albuquerque?"

The Silver City.

Question: "Mesa?"

They'll rename it Phoenix.

Question: "Denver?"

The Golden Port.

Question: "Fargo?"

Opportunity.

Question: "Kansas City?"

The Open City.

Question: "St. Louis?"

City of Purity.

Question: "Memphis?"

That stays the same.

Question: "How about Dallas?"

It will be on the edge of the delta.

Question: "The little island that's left in the Bay of Reconciliation?"

The Island of Vision.

Question: "Detroit?"

Achilles.

CHAPTER TWELVE
with Saint Germain and Kuthumi

From the Heart

*"What is the use of the Mental Body without
the qualities of Divine Compassion and Divine Love?"*
- EL MORYA

Today Saint Germain and Kuthumi have opened up the portal of communication through divine thanks and appreciation. From their own Heart Chakras, a beam is projecting out that goes right to my own I AM Presence. They are saying that this is important, and enables communication with anyone we want to communicate with.

A TECHNIQUE FOR HEALING AND PHYSICAL MANIFESTION

Saint Germain is showing me how you can use, with your hands, the same Vortex of energy they had directed from their Heart Chakras to my Higher Self. The same energy flows into the center of the hand. You can direct if for healing or you could direct it for protection. You can direct it for whatever need you have, even for prosperity. Use your right hand only. You hold your hand out and visualize what you want.

Then you take you left hand and cover your heart and ask for the divine highest good.

Question: "Is the power in doing this proportional to our faith and belief in it?"

He says to see yourself as the Vortex and know that you yourself are the Vortex. Or through the use of the circle, standing within the circle, is one way you can do this too. Kuthumi does this through meditation. Saint Germain does it though precipitation. Whatever you wish to individualize.

We have to change, and we have to be willing to accept changes in order to precipitate whatever we meditate upon.

CHAPTER THIRTEEN
with Saint Germain and Sananda

Choice

"Stand firm when you make a choice."
- SAINT GERMAIN

THE CLEANSING AND THE LAW OF ATTRACTION

The surface of this planet has offered herself to assist in the cleansing of the lower bodies of mankind and bring to the surface all that needs to be brought forth, dispensed, and dispelled for this age of time. Yes, during this age you have seen the pillage and the rape of people, but you must understand the accountability of these people for their actions. You can only attract to yourself what you have brought into your being through your own self.

This will be the greatest teaching to mankind during this time, the acceptance of responsibility for their location during these Earth Changes. What you attract may indicate what needs to be spun away, spun off, as you would call it, from the source of your soul. Perhaps persons are tempted to steal and what better way for them to take this quality from their lower self but to be in the position where they may be allowed to do so. Or perhaps, they will be given the opportunity to be stolen from.

Do you not see, Dear ones, this is the choice we make. We are learning and teaching that the responsible use of our own energy is but a call to the higher Christ Self, to the Beloved Mighty I AM Presence! Through this call, you take the eternal protection of the Blue-White Flame with Archangel Michael. Beloved Archangel Michael has come and has bound all foreign entities from your Earth Planet and Plane at this time. So the entities that you encounter are those which have been created only through the thought and feeling world of mankind.

HIGHER VIBRATION, LOVE, AND FORGIVENESS

This is the true choice for humanity, to experience good and bad, lightness and darkness and see eternal love. For the experiment in the next ten years is to show mankind the eternal truths, the truth which will never leave the face of this planet. For as the vibration moves up into the higher fourth stage, mankind will experience The Constants.

Let me outline these for you, please. Constant One, the Law of Love. Constant Two, the Law of Mercy and Forgiveness. Constant Three, the Application of Universal Principles. Let me further explain that the Third Constant is built and applied only through the first two. The Earth is not exclusive in its contract and agreement with this universe, for there are many other planets which have entered into similar contract and agreement.

You see, Dear ones, as you experience the third to the fourth reality, or transition, on the Earth Plane and Planet, you will see that throughout the universe other planets have been built upon the same principles, or third Constant. The Earth is not exclusive in its suffering and many of the planets have chose as she has. They send their Ray of Divine Compassion towards the Earth Plane and the Planet at this time.

Perhaps the planet which suffered even greater was Mars. For, you see, the masculine qualities of the planet Mars allowed for horrendous crimes, not only to the physical body but to the spiritual. They had developed ways to actually enter into the finer bodies and continue the combat. But it was through the recognition of the Divine Vibration, the first Constant, Love, which altered this planet's path. This divine vibration, which serves also as a universal principle, remains throughout this universe.

You must understand love as being an energy. It is the substance of which all is composed and built upon. And the opposite of this energy is the energy of fear and doubt. For love is the ability for the individual to trust. This is the vibration with which we continue to work as we develop our bonds of trust with you and give our eternal assistance and support. For the next lesson that mankind will learn is the ability to assist and support one another. For what they are learning is that the energy Vibration of Love is to be extended. Yes, perhaps, this does seem to be a simple explanation and yes, indeed, it is harder to act upon. But these are the eternal truths and Constants that you must practice!

SUSTAINING LOVE THROUGH THE PRACTICE OF THE VIOLET FLAME

I would like to address the principle of the Violet Flame of which we discussed earlier. The Violet Flame is a practice that you may come to understand as sustaining the eternal energy of love. Through the experience and use of this bonded energy, you learn Divine Acceptance of the self as it is. You do not experience the turmoil to the same degree as if you are not using the Violet Flame.

What a great work this has been for the Planetary Council to bring the dispensation of the Violet Flame to mankind! To experience and use Mercy, Forgiveness, Divine Compassion, and Grace, you then extend this to others. The Violet Flame is not only an exclusive contract made between you and the Higher Self, it is a contract which is made and extended to the world about you. As you carry the flame about your body, its ability to transcend all problems is extended to others around you.

And so Dear ones, in the use of the Violet Flame remember there are the Divine Principles and the use of the three times three. For as you enter into the contract of using the Violet Flame, it is the law that touches the lives and extends into the hearts of others. This happens not only through oral communication but perhaps you will just be walking and feel the Violet Flame about you. Others will look at you and exclaim, 'What is it about this person? What is this feeling I have for this person?" It is the Violet Flame. It is the use of the Law of Mercy.

So you see Dear ones, through the use of this eternal law you are able to extend it on to others. This is a concept which you've been exposed to and know as synergy, the collective energetic effort of the mass. This is truly what is needed to move the Earth easily into its evolutions. For the Earth is prepared to harmonize the Green Ray with the Violet Ray. How can this happen but through the assistance of its inhabitants, those who have become a part of her are now her.

Are not your bodies composed of that of the earth elements itself? Have not you used her energy for a time? Extend the Violet Flame to her! For this is the dispensation of the Violet Flame in its approach to the Earth Plane. Let the Violet Flame come through the channels of the God-Beings that inhabit her surface!

And now I'll open the floor for questions.

Question: "We were wondering what our tasks are to be now as we start working together again. Is it to put out the world map or to continue with the products? What would be the priority?"

CHOICE REFLECTS OUR TRUE MOTIVATIONS

Yes, we have work for you to do, as we have always said that there is much to do to continue your work within the light. But we have stressed to you the Laws of Commitment. Stand firm when you make your choice. There is work to do and it must stand as ONE body of work.

We commend and applaud you for what you have achieved, for it has been a monumental task to step as far as you have stepped. It has been a monumental leap to leave what you feel is conventional, to raise your vibration to this level and to extend this to mankind. We applaud you and thank you for the tremendous effort and work. We will continue to dispense the work as you ask and are willing, for, you see, we are not allowed to infringe upon the free will. Through this you will team the responsibility of your energies. For is not the understanding of this work the understanding of the power of the Beloved Mighty I AM working within your life? Perhaps you do not understand how strong this power is. It is a tremendous force, a tremendous force which works on the principle of attraction. Do you understand?

Response: "No, please explain."

He's writing on the board. He has written, "Commitment -> Agreement -> Choice -> Responsibility -> Action -> Life Force."

As you see this chart, Dear ones, do you not understand all of your actions come with the original commitment and the original agreement which you have made. Your actions are your true motivations. Does this clarify?

Response: "Yes, I think so."

Wonderful! This is truly magnificent! You see, Dear one, this is the way we have interacted with you. We are not allowed to enter into your consciousness for your upliftment without the action of your choice and without the motivation of your pure heart.

Response: "I've been very aware of how my motivation or intent has changed over the last year or two."

Good! Your ability to recognize is your ability to carry on the contract with us. Who are we but an extension of the people in your life! We are not allowed to come into the physical during this transitional time, but our work is being carried out through those whom we call our messengers. And no, we have not positioned them to be glorified, but you must come to the realization that all those within your life are truly messengers! For our energies are of Service and benefit to all.

Your ability to keep your agreement with those about you is important and you must understand this law. This is the true way that we function and communicate. We have formed agreements with you in order to even speak with you. This agreement is made through the Higher Self. Your choice is to have this experience. All that is, is through choice, and the responsibility of choice is yours.

THE NATURAL LAW OF RESPONSIBILITY

Were the intent and motivation of the great Alpha and the Omega to create this energy and then disharmonize it through unbalanced dependence, such lack of responsibility would destroy the original intent. The original intent is for the energy to be like that in the parent and to take on the creative qualities inherent of the parent. So yes, you see the similarity of the energy, and now the energy must learn to be responsible unto itself. For in the same way the bird is hatched from the egg and nurtured and loved and cared for within the nest, until the time arrives for it to fly. And what does this bird do, but at the next springtime, nest again.

This example from nature has been brought to you to show you the creative universal principle. It is by no mistake and design that she is there for you to observe. She brings to the simplest levels the true examples. It is the work of the Elemental Life Force to bring universal principles to the physical level. Observe and watch! For mankind will soon be shoved from his nest and must learn to accept the responsibility, his Divine Similarity, what his parent insured in his code!

We would like to take a break at this moment to allow you to contemplate this. Do you have any questions?

Response: "No."

There is music playing.

We bring the music of the planet to you. The Elemental Life plays as violins in the world symphony! As these birds do sing, and the winds blow, and the sun beats its warmth upon your heart, this is the symphony of cooperation. And where has this cooperation come from but through agreement. Do you understand?

Response: "Yes."

And now Beloved Sananda will speak.

Yes, I come to the planet to beg of you to continue this work. I come to you to offer the cup again, to drink and to sup with me! For remember me in the last supper when I indeed broke bread with my Brothers. This is what we beg of you. Break this bread. Break this light work which you are called to share and extend it to your Brothers.

There are many ways in which you may do this Service, that you know as healing one another. But, understand that you are truly never separated from the source. As you feel your wings, as you are pushed from the nest, fly with your Brothers. Sup with them. For the twelve years of transition have begun and we have called to you to arm yourself with the Principles of Forgiveness. I have said to you, I and the Father are ONE. And this I truly say, that you and I are ONE. I AM Sananda. You and your Brother are truly ONE. Recognize and sup with him.

Saint Germain steps forward.

Yes, there is work to be done, and there are Earth Change Maps which can be completed, and we are willing to dispense the information. First, the Central American countries. Second, South America. Third, what you call Canada. If you would like to take this work, this is the order which we wish you to study.

Response: "Okay."

Acquaint yourself. And now I say to you Dear Brother, call to the Violet Flame as a call to the heart. I ask you to love and bless one another and to extend this flame from my heart to yours and then to others. I AM Saint Germain.

CHAPTER FOURTEEN
with Saint Germain and Sananda

With Love

"I AM a loving Mother and I enfold you in my love and care."
- MOTHER MARY

JOURNEY INTO THE SEVENTH CYCLE

Saint Germain is holding my hand and we're traveling. I look down and can see the tops of mountains and canyons below. This is very beautiful. He says, "Acquaint yourself." Sananda is on my right hand side, and he begins to speak.

Send this message to the Earth with love. I have spoken to you of the twelve years of changes. Our work now begins. It is time to complete another phase of this body of work. We impart this information to all who are ready and willing to receive it. We could give you more discourse and information on personal growth and relationship; however, we feel compelled at this time to complete this work so an understanding of the Earth's journey, her soul growth, is gained and imparted to mankind.

For many epochs we have seen this tale. And it is time to complete the most crucial cycle, the seventh cycle. Beloved Saint Germain has been assigned to give you the details. I AM the first messenger for the Earth Plane and Planet that many have known as Terra. For I was here at her beginning, and I will be here as she completes this great birth. For the beginning was the conception and now, since the conception and birth, it is time for you to walk. It is time for you to stand and to take your steps. Do you understand this message that I bring to you?

Response: "Yes."

Now for the completion of information I turn the floor to Beloved Saint Germain.

Greetings chelas. As you complete your Fifth Ray work, the ministry of Service to mankind, there are times that you are weary. See that this extension of the Service that you give to others is truly a healing process for yourself. For as you complete this work, you too become complete. I AM here! I AM always with you in Service with the Divine Plan! We open the floor for your questions.

Response: "I have no questions."

The question has been addressed about Earth Changes and the dispensation of information. There are many theories on your plane about the opening of windows and of portals. You see, Dear ones, there are select ones which open and select ones which we must close, for the dispensation of information does indeed occur along the Vibration of Harmony.

This information is accessed through like vibration. Consciously project, through Harmony, to the open door to access this information. This has happened as another approach during the hours of sleep, but now you extend this activity to your waking hours and learn the value of developing consciousness. Let us continue this work of Earth Changes. You have asked, " Why has this come at this time?" Do you not know, Dear ones, that this work comes as you are ready for it. Do you not understand that as you are willing, you will receive?

Response: "I have understood the growth that we needed to make before we could be receiving this next step."

PROPHECY, FEAR, AND THE DIMENSION OF LOVE

Not only is there growth, but there must be sincere willingness, the desire to use this information for constructive means. And so we open the portal for the information of Central America, but first I give you this visualization. As you have seen the pillars which have stood on the United States, you too must see these pillars which stand across the Central countries of America. For again, this work is built on a clear vision, on a foundation. We must hold and always maintain focus for the end result.

In this work of Prophecy, much fear can be instilled among the hearts of man. You must hold this vision that this completion brings a completion to the dream. The vision brings love. And as these strategic points are set up, you will begin to understand the theories of lei-lines, portals, windows, and the many labels that you have used for classification of access to the Fourth Dimension. I open the floor for you to direct your questions regarding upcoming changes of the Mexico coastline; for, as you recall, we are here for your assistance.

BAJA, MEXICO

Question: "I have already seen a large bay formed on the West side of the upper part of Mexico and this is drawn on the map we are working on. Will the Baja area remain or will that sink with the bay?"

The bay to be formed shall be given the name Bay of Divinity for its alignment with the trinity. I shall give you the measurements from the beginning which you have penned on the map, 1700. A measurement given in kilometers, and then several degrees directly to the south. The information is accurate regarding the Diamond Islands and you shall see the scattering of these islands.

He is showing a high ridge coming up over the islands in the Baja area. There is a central ridge extending down the center, but it will occur in a different time period.

Question: "Is this after the changes have stopped?"

He is showing that after the islands erode, there'll be some sort of shift or earth movement, and this ridge will rise up again. It's covered by water at the present moment. After the islands are completely eroded the ridge will shift up.

This bay area will extend on into present Mexico, approximately 85 kilometers.

Question: "Will that new mountain ridge touch the main coast?"

This is to be a new island, formed for the Golden Age.

Response: "Okay."

The area is to be called Resurrection Island and on it will be a newly formed mountain range. For truly, at that point, mankind shall feel the resurrection of his true self! This area of which we speak was at one time the birth land for another civilization.

Question: "That called Mu?"

That is somewhat accurate. Remnants of the Mu civilization helped in the colonization.

He's showing me what it was like.

This is pre-Atlantis.

Response: "Okay."

THE YUCATAN

On the East Coast a new ridge raises. This is a plate formation with that of the Cooperation Mountains. These mountains extend under the ocean waters, the tip coming into the central part. For you see, this is a mountain range which will follow not only through the United States but the Central States and down into South America. The shift of the planetary plate will form this mountain range which we now see. Do you have questions?

He has taken the Earth and split it in half and is showing how this range comes into being. I can see the range. I can visualize it making an S curve.

Question: "And does it go right on down out into the Yucatan?"

Yes, this area, the Yucatan area, is to be raised. While you look at this you would imagine that it would sink. This is not so, for this is the gift that we give to this great peninsula, to this area of the Earth which sponsored, as you have recalled, the civilization of Mu.

CHAPTER FIFTEEN
with Kuthumi

Dance of the Circle

*"Offer forgiveness to one another,
and the Mother offers hers."*
- MOTHER MARY

THE ELEMENTAL LIFE OF FOURTH DIMENSION

I'm seeing a spinning light that forms a circle. It's like a fire, a glowing light, and I walk in.

I AM Kuthumi and I have opened this portal to you from the fire center of the Earth Planet! My work is with Elemental Life, known as the Dance of the Circle. This Elemental, called the Salamander of Fire, is a light, best described in your physical expression as the fire of creative energy. The work of the elements is the synthesis of creative force! This is a process of cooperation, and the focus of creative force is to interact together to produce an end result. I AM focusing this energy of Elemental love!

I have spoken to you regarding our Brothers who will work in this portion of the Earth Planet which you have called Mexico. We refer to it as a land known as "the bridge." For in this area you will experience the true work of becoming the bridge. Many will be led to this area during your Time of Transition and experience the empowerment of the bridge. This is first perceived as sightings of UFOs or light ships. And clearly this is the focus of our Elemental energies performing a function of Third to Fourth and Fourth to Third (Dimension).

Many who have what you call the psychic abilities will be drawn to this area for the convention of 1991.

[Editor's Note: This is a prophecy of the 1991 UFO sightings in Mexico.]

This is an open invitation! For those who wish to learn the process of projected consciousness, what has been known as in your time as channel is indeed a bridge. Project yourself from your Earthly point of view! Bridge yourself to a New Dimension.

So what is this work with the Elementals and how does it relate to what I now tell you? You see, my Dear hearts, each of the Elemental Life Forces: earth, wind, fire, water, are there not four? Each represents an aspect from Fourth Dimension manifest in a Third Dimensional composite. I sense you have questions.

Response: "No."

Let us address the circle. What is the circle of creative fire? Let the four elements unite!

He's showing me how they spin together and form a circle.

Yes, this is the dance of life! For you see inherent in this Elemental Life the qualities which you recall from the Fourth Dimension pulled apart. No, not separated, differentiated. This is what the planet has exampled. She has differentiated Fourth Dimension! Earth representing the Universal Principle of Stability. Water representing the Universal Principle of Movement. Fire representing the Universal Principle of Bonding. Do you understand?

Response: "Yes."

Air brings creative movement. Fire changes and transforms. Water moves continually. Earth is unchanged and stable. These are Elemental Principles from which you must learn not to be separated, but differentiated, and then integrate them again into ONE. Do you see this in your Elemental Life world? In trees, in what you term plant life? In animal life? The weather Devas? The Mineral Kingdom? All of this has been sorted and differentiated, and is now coming to completion and being reunited. What a great Service this has been from the planet to you. What a great Service this has been from the plane to the planet!

VOLCANIC ACTIVITY

Now I would like to speak of the volcanic activities in the area of the bridge.

Now he's showing me that all along the eastern side there's a mountain ridge, and much volcanic activity.

Soon creative force comes to stabilize! Do you have questions?

He is now showing the interplay of the elements in this area.

A lot of washing and cleansing from water. Again, the upper corner experiencing the four elements totally. Water, earth, fire, air, lots of wind. Water rushing. Volcanic activity.

Question: "The volcanic activity will extend from the border of the United States clear to Mexico City?"

His map shows that it turns, goes to the tip of the Yucatan. There's some mountain ridge on the eastern side and sinking of the land from the mountain ridge into just a narrow strip.

Question: "Then the mountain ridge east will sink?"

128 kilometers, to the Yucatan. The Yucatan is completely covered and flooded. Not sunk, he's saying flooded. He'd like that word to be used, flooded.

Question: "Tidal wave?"

He's saying precisely monsoon winds, high wind. It's a warm wind; it's not a cold wind, it's a warm wind.

Question: "Is it the volcanic activity setting up these tremendous wind forces coming in, that changes the weather this radically?"

It will be perceived as such but it is truly the weather Devas performing this function. This allows the Elementals to unite into ONE creative force! For in opening up this area a great alignment with the stellar bodies occurs. And this alignment now bridges to other planets.

Question: "So I take it most of this will happen at a later time?"

THE TIME OF TRANSITION

This is the Time of Transition. There is not one event but twelve years of events. You do not have one major cataclysm. This is twelve years of transition.

I'm also seeing a great light coming. Another meteorite that hits in the ocean area.

Question: "It's in the Gulf of Mexico?"

Near the Yucatan. In the ocean.

See the waters coming! I would like to use the word again to you, "flooding."

Question: "Does the meteorite hit on the West or East side?"

East.

Response: "Okay. And that creates the tidal wave and the rains."

Flooding, ash fall, flooding, volcanic activity, flooding; these are the events that I show you. I AM Kuthumi.

CHAPTER SIXTEEN
with Mother Mary, Kuthumi,
Saint Germain, Kuan Yin, and Paul

Heartland

"You must now serve the planet as your Sister."
- SANANDA

Beloved Mary speaks.

We will nurture you. Extend these gifts. Walk along this path of light. Trust in me. From the four directions I AM come, from the winds, from four directions. Dear heart, a heart that beats as mine, this message to your soul: FEAR NOT, THERE IS GREAT JOY! Feel this Mother planet move and heave and you will feel this movement move forward. A PLANET HEALED!

THE PROCESS OF BECOMING

Beloved Kuthumi enters.

In completion, do you not see how 144 could merge to become ONE collective unit? We know this is quite an impossible task for you, as human beings, to understand, for even the merging of your spirit into itself is quite a challenge! To merge with another and then to merge as the seven is the next step! At ten this group collective consciousness merges into ONE. You may see this as quite invasive, and yet, Dear ones, it is the most uplifting. For in the soul units is contained human collective consciousness; but you see, Elemental Life also evolves and merges with this collective consciousness.

I send this message to you so you may understand a deeper reality. Understand, the planet which you walk upon has felt human emotion. It is performing this task, is brought to this point. Feel hope in the midst of despair! Feel the great joy, for you too shall have this opportunity! You ask yourself, when is this time? Soon, you will begin to understand, Dear ones, there is no time. There is only the I AM, which Is. For all moves forward seeking growth and joy! Do not feel yourself separated. Do not think yourself separated. For this is a process and all play their part in their role. Enjoy the dance, for this is truly what it is! An expression of life eternal. Do you have questions?

Response: "Yes, I'm beginning to feel more of the joy and the connection with the groups than previously. I can see the mirror between the Earth's movements and ours."

Do you not feel the movement of your soul into a larger reality? For this is truly what we extend to you as the energy of love. Say openly to one another, I love you. Say and express openly to one another, I accept you. Say openly and express to one another, I AM you. For this is what we speak of, Fourth Dimensional conception.

As you move towards one another, into groups of cooperative, collective consciousness, many of these groups will be known as soul clusters. For as you merge together you find a collective purpose for that of which I AM becoming! This is the structure of movement, or magnetism, as you understand it in your physical world. Drawing to yourself what you are, and drawing away what must be spun off from yourself, the positive draws and attaches to the positive; but the positive and the negative repel one another. So they break and force themselves away from one another. They then seek and then find likeness and are united again and seen as ONE. Do you understand, Dear heart?

Response: "Yes, I do. I think the challenge to communicate this to others is the concept of positive and negative being both good, and that it's not one extreme or the other but a series of levels all in between."

It is most wonderful that you have seen this. For, as you see, even in what you perceive as negative, the attraction to one another serves a great purpose in the Divine Plan. The soul clusters modulate together, and then form as a separate unit with collective thought and movement. This movement is an emergence. Emergence is the most simple way to understand resurrection. Emergence is a movement based on universal principles. Resurrection is an energetic movement which seeks and finds commitment. Universal principles underly both activities.

You must understand, we give you these concepts and principles in their most simple forms for you to understand. Yes, there are periods of stillness that you experience. You question the effectiveness of simplicity, but we must impress on you universal principle finds its means through the mind and its ends in the soul. As this is applied and experienced, you further the movement to your Emotional Body, through your Mental Body, and to the spiritual or finer bodies, for this is where lasting creation is impressed.

To suppress the Emotional Body, to suppress the Mental Body, the impression is not clear, for you see, the experience of creative movement is not present. Through movement, the chakra, or energy centers, are impressed. You carry this momentum to the Resurrection Body, and this is the collective body which you truly carry with you to Fourth and Fifth Dimensions and on to the higher dimensional realities. Emergence/Ressurrection becomes the acceptance of experience.

Allow experience to flow and to move through you. See yourself as the Chalice of Life. See yourself as a Cup that the mighty I AM Presence and the mighty I AM experiences pour through. Ready yourself to drink this life! See these experiences harmonizing, uniting you into the ONE. Do you understand?

Response: "Yes."

And now, to continue this work, this project, I am bringing for my assistance those who have been commanded. May I introduce to you the Chohan of the Americas, Beloved Saint Germain, who has sponsored the Americas through Divine Principle. He is the light-bearer bringing the wisdom of the East and the teachings of the East to the Western world. There is much misunderstanding of his position and place. But, Dear ones, I ask for you to see and appreciate all that he has individualized. That is the Flame of Freedom! And this is the experience which is occurring in the Western Hemisphere, for it was founded upon the principles of religious freedom. But you must understand the underlying Divine Principle. You have incarnated in the Americas to fully express freedom, and what a Divine Right this is! And now I bring to you Saint Germain.

THE FLAME OF FREEDOM

Greetings chelas. I AM honored with the introduction from my Brother and friend. It is love and compassion, expressed through the Flame of Freedom, that Beloved Kuthumi uses as a Flame of Action! The Flame of Freedom expresses the Flame of True Motivation. For do you not see, without free choice you have excluded universal principle? The principle of freedom is what the western world is to be built upon. I am honored to be given this position.

I would like to introduce the others who have come, offering their assistance, and who would like to speak regarding our Service. For you see, Dear ones, this Project of Transition is Beloved Sananda's, known as Jesus from your Earth history. And his work as this figure now merges with the Violet

Flame. With us are those who have built upon the principles of the Violet Flame. Beloved Kuan Yin whose work with the Pink Ray is complete. Beloved Paul whose assistance has also completed her work. They are present to share Divine Compassion and Divine Love with the planet. Understand the energy of love. We bring to you the lessons of Compassion, Love, Mercy, and Forgiveness. All are built on the foundation called the energy of love. They are the principles which express and expand the energy of love. And now I turn the floor over to Beloved Kuan Yin.

THE MOTHER'S HEART AND THE FIRST RACE

I AM the fellowship of the heart. I come to you to bring Earth Change information and I call to you to understand the Heart of the Mother. For you see, this area on which we now work was indeed the Motherland, the area which originally sponsored many of the first embodiments and incarnations of those who came to serve. I come to serve and extend love to this Earth. Through her grateful heart, she gave. So we now address the Yucatan peninsula, that area which shall go underwater to cleanse. We have said to you it shall rise again, and it shall be so. Under the waters for 200 years, with the raising of what you call the Cooperation Mountains she shall be raised again as a great monument to the first race.

I shall speak to you of this first race, which you will now recall for you were both there; a race created not only from this Earth but from the call to the universe. Through sound and universal principle your body was formed and it merged with the Earth as a collective consciousness. This is known as the transmitting and the transmuting of matter. You called for the energy vibration to enter your form and, as it entered, you merged with the Earth energies and densified to this dimension. Do you understand?

Response: "Yes."

And so this area of the Yucatan is most precious to me for it serves as the Heart of the Mother. Surrounding her precious heart shall be a fresh-water sea. For, as these mountains rise, the fresh water shall be restored. I would like for you to observe her most southern area. For the salt water shall be around her for a time but, as the chain of mountains emerges, this shall rise and a beautiful inland fresh-water sea shall be formed. Its Service will be as a mirror to many. Would you like some measurements?

Response: "Please."

DEEP WITHIN AND THE LAKE OF MIRRORS

This fresh-water sea shall extend from the Yucatan down to the tip of what is known as Brazil. This clear, placid, fresh-water sea will be named the Lake of Mirrors. Traveling upon its water, people will be able to observe and to see deep within themselves. Under the Lake of Mirrors are many caverns that extend to the inner Earth. The motherly, earthly energies merge with collective universal thought at this lovely fresh-water scene. You see, Dear ones, it is charged neither negatively nor positively. Her water comes for you to observe only as a gift from the inner Earth. Seek neither to qualify one way or the other, but for that energy which clearly seeks growth and experience. It shall be neither a resort nor commercial area. It shall be for one seeking the inner, one who seeks to go within. Mankind at that time shall recognize it as such, and it shall be set aside into a great reserve. Down to the tip of Brazil see this lake!

CENTRAL AMERICA

To the West side, the chain of land in Central America shall remain. While some coastal activity will upset it, a thin strip will remain. At no time will the Americas suffer the cutting of the cord, for they are one and the same. North America and South America were, indeed, at one time twin flames. This area of Central America is the bridge, the cord which is the link. To the West side, you will see much of this land broken into islands, but a mountain range will remain as the link, and form the eastern coast for the Lake of Mirrors.

Question: "Is this fresh water lake fed by both continents or just South America?"

This fresh-water lake will be fed by glacier movement and a quick melting of ice. We know this is difficult for you to understand, Dear ones. I will take my leave at this moment for I wish you to sketch this down to gain greater clarity, and will open the floor again.

I'm seeing the mountains. They are very steep and seem to grow straight out of this bridge!

Question: "Straight out of the water?"

They are extremely high.

Question: "Do you see all the glaciers?"

They're almost covered with ice. They resemble crystals coming right out of the Earth.

Greetings from the Flame of the Heart, I AM Paul. I have come so that you may embrace the fullness of the message we impart to you. I am here for your assistance and ask for your agreement for me to impart my message to you.

Response: "Yes, we are anxious and grateful."

I, too, am grateful. I, too, am filled with awe and inspiration for what you will see in this time period. I am here to impart to you the knowledge of the eternal heart. I would like to give a brief history of myself as an entity speaking to you so you may closely examine my energies. For I am working closely in this area.

I AM Paul. I AM a portion of the light center associated with the Pink Ray, known also as the Heart Ray; for, you see, in this mirror of lakes we embrace the nature of the soul! My homeland at one time was a planet which was pink in nature and had around it three suns. The worship of the sun energy was a common religion for many epochs. Now my home is Terra, for this is where I have ascended. You see, the planet to which you ascend and enter from Fourth to Fifth Dimensional reality becomes your true Motherland. I have spent my time traveling back to the solar system of Quantain, and now I have returned to my true Motherland, which at this time you know as Terra. Since my work is that of carrying the heart light on the western ridge, we shall talk about the changes on the West Coast.

Now he's showing me a very rugged coastline on the western side.

REAPPEARANCE OF THE MASTER

This ridge shall symbolize the silver cord which attaches you to your Higher Self. This ridge now attaches North America to South America! During the Time of Change and Transition, navigation as you know it will be impossible between the two, but remember at the end of the cleanse, the transition, we shall come to bring our eternal assistance. For the bridge is truly a bridging area. For now, we come to you, bridging through Fourth Dimension.

There will be a short period of time where, through cosmic activity, we shall be allowed to bridge in third dimension, a short period, equal to roughly twenty years of Earth time as you know it presently. Do not forget the theories of compaction of time. As you go through the inner transition of Third to Fourth, remember there will come a period of choice.

Do not forget the timeliness of these events. Each is ordered, in a sense, as you are ordered. Each is created as you are created. Remember, I AM Paul, and represent the eternal Heart of Love. You and this planet are indeed eternal in the eyes of God, the Creator. You, on this Earth Plane, may offer yourself as a bridge. Bridge yourself in Service! Bridge yourself in Service to the eternal Heart of the Mother, the eternal Heart of Brotherhood, the Eternal Heart of the Divine Plan!

CHAPTER SEVENTEEN
with Saint Germain

Trust

"Do you see the great circle which opens when you realize that you are ONE with the Elemental Life?"
- SANANDA

Welcome Beloved chelas. I am here for your questions and refinement!

Question: "Am I correct in perceiving from these sketches that this lake will be in the shape of a heart?"

You are correct, and we send the message with the joy of recognition that this eternal heart of the Third Dimension represents transformation in the Fourth Dimension and inspiration in the Fifth Dimension. Within the Earth itself there are large fresh-water lakes underneath this area of South America which shall open to feed the eternal Lake of Mirrors.

Question: "Do these underwater lakes have special properties from the minerals?"

BEYOND DUALITY AND THE I AM PRESENCE

This was exactly and precisely what I was ready to discuss with you, for the Elemental Life Forces which have been withheld until this time, will be released, and their open emergence and cooperation with the eternal hearts of man will truly be realized. For long, these waters of pristine, pure thought have been withheld. Since these waters carry neither a negative nor a positive magnetic charge, they serve with clarity and clearness. They are charged with pure life force, and the individual life force of Elemental water is able to express for this time. Do you understand?

Response: "Yes, it'll have a similar effect to what the extra energies are having on us now."

Do you not understand, Dear ones, that we too feel the extra energies? You may perceive that we are responsible for these energy forces but while we are the transmitters of this energy, we are still not the source. We serve in willing cooperation! You must understand that there are things we still work to understand.

I would like to talk to you on the concept of trust, for trust is acceptance.

TRUST THE PRESENCE

Trust is the open door to honesty. Trust is fully embraced in safety and protection. Where does this safety and protection come from but through the acceptance of trust in the Mighty I AM Presence. The Lake of Mirrors is this symbol. Many perceive it as the safe harbor. Many will travel to find a portion of themselves which they have not yet had an opportunity to see. For at one time, around this great lake which emerges again, and was once connected to the Yucatan, was the land mass known as Africa. You see, it truly was a Motherland and a Heartland as you recall it. But, for this time, my energies shall be directed to the West Coast.

I perceive the East side as the side that could be travelled to connect the North and the South and more on the physical, and then the West side as more the spiritual.

The West, geographically, is rugged and non-navigable. You must perceive this side as being like a dike or a dam that holds back the salt seas. It is the East which will be navigated by foot.

During the transition, there will be areas of extreme sinking, to the core on the West, sinking to the bedrock core. You may fear that, with the earth movements, the cord will break. But use the energy of trust and faith, which I AM. Remember, I AM Faith!

This is such a delightful work for us! We are filled with joy and harmony at the completion of Central America. Do you understand that the map of this area is close to completion?

Response: "Yes."

I would like for you to sketch this out and bring it back to me for final analysis. I would again emphasize this area as being a Heartland. You have asked the question of Vortex areas within the central states. Perhaps the largest Vortex area will be contained within the Lake of Mirrors. We are truly filled with joy. I AM Saint Germain.

CHAPTER EIGHTEEN
with Saint Germain, Kuthumi,
El Morya, and Sananda

Loving Prayer

> *"Send your loving prayers from your
> loving heart to the Earth at this time."*
> - KUTHUMI

Greetings chelas. I AM Saint Germain, and I step forward to impress on you the lessons and the information you may differentiate to dispense in your physical world. I bring to you the other pillars, Beloved Kuthumi and Beloved El Morya, for they have come to speak this day. I would like to allow them to take the floor this morning.

Welcome, I AM Kuthumi.

I AM flowing with everlasting life!
I AM the giver of the waters of life!
I AM the giver of the fire of the flame!
I AM within the winds that change!
I AM the spirit of the Earth that holds the vessel and the Golden Cup!
I AM a receiver of light!
I AM come so that you may have life in its fullest!

YOU ARE ONE WITH THE EARTH

Beloveds, do you see the great circle which opens when you realize that you are ONE with the Elemental Life? The continuous completion of the circle expresses with Elemental Life as the Dance of Life! Within each of these the I AM, the God source, is in full expression. It is indeed, individualized, and yet ONE with the source, and works in harmony and with cooperation. This is the work I have been assigned during the Time of Transition. The importance of the impression of this thought is expedient! The vessel cries in its discomfort. We must harmonize with the source for the waters are agitated, the winds speak with violence, the fires urge to burn with destructive passion. The Earth cries nervously, "This is more than I can bear! This is more than I can bear!"

You who walk upon the plane, you who are here to bond your energy with this Earth Planet, I beg of you to send your loving prayers from your loving heart to the Earth at this time. I beg of you to do this daily, if possible. For you see, this relieves her stress and discomfort. Give to her your support, as you would go to a friend in need. It is time for you to befriend the planet, to embrace her from the source of your loving soul. Now I have information to impart but it is only through your approval for we are not allowed to infringe upon your free will. Does this meet with your approval?

Response: "We are anxious for you to share with us."

I am most anxious to become ONE with you and your consciousness. I would like to impart to you the knowledge of the Circle of Fires. We have spoken of the circle and its fiery dance. This bonds Elemental Life Force into a Vortex or a Circle of Energy. Upon your planet you have this Ring of Fire located upon your Earth Planet maps. I would like to focus on the center of this Circle of Fire. Find this, for within this center, the apex of the Circle of Fire, is the linear position for alignment with Elemental Life upon this planet. This is a center where one may bond through universal laws shared in the galaxies with other Elemental Life forms. Do you understand?

Question: "Yes. This is at the Heart Chakra?"

It is much different from the Heart Chakra, for this energy point is related to collective consciousness of the Earth Planet. This information I impart to you is related to the Elemental Life Force which inhabits the Earth Planet and yet has played a composite role for the Earth Planet. Does this clarify?

Response: "Yes."

I would like for you to study this location for it is the operative center from which my web is woven. Remember the numerical value of the number four is related to Fourth Dimension reality, for Elemental Life Force operates consciously at Fourth Dimension and has exclusively bonded itself to the third. I would like to share this location of the circle with you, so in our work together you will understand weather patterns on the planet. Through this understanding, you then learn how time is calculated. For you see, Dear ones, is not time the interaction of Elemental Life Force and the measurement of this interaction? Do you understand?

Response: "Yes."

I AM the balanced love of Earth, I AM Kuthumi.

He steps back and Saint Germain is coming forward.

Beloved Brothers of the Flame, I would like to introduce to you my Brother and comrade, El Morya. This Beloved one has worked for truth and wisdom and its application through the Mental Body at this time on the Earth Plane. For you, too, must understand the work of the body of the planet at this time. Who more concisely may explain it than he?

DETACH FROM EGO THROUGH THE DIVINE WILL

Welcome, I AM El Morya. I come to you in strength and courage. I come to you to impart to you the wisdom of the Will of God. Let me clarify. What is this Will that we have spoken of? The will can be that of ego orientation, and yet has this not served a purpose? Has this not served a purpose for the Earth Planet? Surrounding your Earth are several layers. Each layer corresponds exactly to a layer of the human body. At the third layer around the Earth is the belt associated with the will ego, which is closely related in your physical sense to magnetism and theories of electricity. This is similar in the human embodiment, for it is charged negatively or positively. Do you understand?

Response: "Yes."

Let me take this one step further. The challenge is to sustain a neutral position so that you may become a clear receiver of light. It is the same with the Earth Planet so she may become a clear receiver of light. Now, let us discuss interference with this belt. For you see, Dear ones, while the ego has served a purpose in patterning a charge of protection for survival, it has also set up a magnetic, invasive charge, thus your thoughts can and have invaded this belt of magnetic energy around the Earth Planet. What must be done to neutralize the charge? Steadily hold the focus. Thy Will be done. Thy Will be done from this God source, the source of light, the source that I AM.

Question: "Is this just a simple meditation?"

Absolutely, this is correct. Just a simple meditation! For you see, the turning of one's highly charged will over to the God source is the neutralization of these ions. You have experienced pollution, and you have experienced much in the physical which does not serve the human on the Earth. My call to you is simple. Be responsible for your actions. Be responsible to the source. This is simple. I have given you the instructions and now I would like to give you further information. As you feel the ions about your body becoming neutralized rays, the energy force bathes your body with its neutral charge. This then allows the Third Eye Chakra to open and you may see clearly what is your ego. Then apply wisdom as a tool. The Mental Body contains the ability to detach, and the ability to program. You must learn to pattern with emotion which is neither negative nor positive, what is detached from charge! Learn to program the Mental Body, charged neither negative nor positive but neutralized, programmed as ONE with the Source. Do you understand?

Response: "Yes."

ONENESS AND DIVINE LOVE

For this is the Will of God and once you have patterned this area of your human existence, you must closely tie it in with the heart. Understand that it is not only through our thought processes that we understand Oneness. What use is the Mental Body without the qualities of Divine Compassion and Divine Love? You must learn the focused, individualized use of vibrational energy, and then work for integration. Do you understand?

Response: "Yes."

I've now explained to you this magnetic layer around the Earth. Please continue your work. If I may be of further assistance, I will be glad to share with you.

Response: "Thank you."

He's stepping back and Saint Germain comes forward.

These two Beloved ones have been appointed to serve on a quadrant commission. We have spoken of the Pillars, the integration of four moving to the synthesis of five. It is important that you understand their individualized works and their position held for twelve years of transition. It is important that your understanding of their work be thorough, and then each has an opportunity to choose. And now I know you have many questions. How may I be of assistance?

Question: The session before last we had trouble with our recorder and we missed your message. Could you repeat it please?

EARTH CLEANSING AND THE NEW DIMENSIONS OF CONSCIOUSNESS

Specifically, my committed message of the Earth cleansing concerns raising from the Fifth Dimension to Seventh Dimension. We have spoken of the Violet Flame and the work of the Planetary Council at this time. You see, Dear ones, timing is crucial, and we give to you our everlasting love and project to you the energy to inspire and direct you to keep you in this work.

Sananda steps forward.

Dear hearts, it is with great joy I come to you. I AM the grateful extension of the kingdom! I AM come to you to extend to you this hand in Service, for this is my message to you: Service to mankind and Service to the planet on the plane of your existence. You must now serve the planet as your Sister.

We have spoken of the collective consciousness which layers the body of the Earth at this time.

We would like for you to observe this collective consciousness and know Earth as your close Sister. Share and sup with your Brothers, sending your energy to her at this time. We have discussed the lesson of duality. Duality mirrors to you for your own cleansing. Do you not see, Dear ones, the instrument which was given to you clearly identifies the Earth Planet and identifies the Earth Plane? The merging of Third and Fourth Dimension contains a pitted area in the area of contact. We've spoken to you about areas of compression and compaction. This contact area is an area of compression and compaction. Do you have further questions?

Question: "No. I have a question on Lori's dream she was given last night. She saw the red skies. Were we waiting in anticipation of going to the weather crystal?"

These red skies are the interaction of the massive amount of ash coming through what we call the electronic belt. You're searching for the pinpoint, called the point of intersection. By understanding the points of interaction, you are able to dissipate large amounts of debris from the atmosphere. This will be part of your work with the product we have given you, locating the strategic points for the cleansing of the atmosphere.

CHAPTER NINETEEN
with Saint Germain and the Angel Archais

Cradleland

*"Resurrection becomes the acceptance of experience.
Allow experience to flow and to move through you."*
- KUTHUMI

Saint Germain is present and he has brought another being with him who has a radiant, golden, flowing essence around him.

I bring to you the Angel Archais, protector of these lands. Archais' role is Service as Divine Director of the Cradle. His presence will embrace the Cradle.

Archais steps forth.

THE ANDES MOUNTAINS

I AM the essence of the light that nurtures what steps forth in the Cradle! I am here to embrace this land, to bring forth its majesty, and impart the understanding of its destiny. Let me impart to you an understanding of the Andes Mountains in Peru. Their Service at one time provided a great focus of light to the seven original civilizations. For you see, they stood in honor of the seven cultures. Their mighty majesty served as receptors and generators of light energy. They indeed broke this energy, and dispensed it to the individualized seven races.

These mountains came not through the emergence of the work of the Earth Planet but through the work of the Earth Plane. From this projected Earth Plane energy, known as Alpha and Omega, came the universal principle, love. A great projection of love they were!

These mountains came to embrace the Cradle. They were indeed a gift of nativity, and so I say to you, they shall remain. They are truly a gift of nativity and thus are named that. For you see, Dear ones, at either end they become what you perceive as islands surrounded by water, and to the South remain embedded within the heart. Please write Nativity upon their face! Emerging from them one will see the powerful crystalline light which they contain. They are indeed a gift, christening the Earth Plane. Do you have questions?

Question: "You're referring to the area of these mountains on the West side of the Lake of Mirrors or farther South in South America?"

I am referring to the mountains upon the West coastline of South America.

Response: "Okay."

I say to you that area which you know is what we refer to as the Land of the Cradle. For it was in this area that those seeking embodiment came to this Earth Plane. There had previously been those seeking embodiment on the Earth Planet, and those who rose up from her and through her. There are those which descended to her and merged their physiology with her. Do you see this distinct difference?

Response: "Yes."

BALANCE AND THE NEW ECONOMY

You must understand the Divine Balance. Do you not perceive two gold balls connected through a shaft of golden light? One representing Earth Planet, another representing the creative source. What is the connecting cord? This represents the dimension that serves between the two. This is referred to as the Plane Dimension. For simplicity we call it the Earth Plane.

There are those who come from the ball, the source known as Alpha/Omega, directly to the Cradle. There are those who have emerged from the center of the heart of Terra and in the beginning were as Terra. They have now emerged from soul unit with the entity from Alpha and Omega. But, Beloved Terra, she had indeed offered to sponsor those who would come from her. There are those who have been sponsored from the direct link of the creative source and those who have brought up their soul, sponsored by those from the heart of Terra. Where is the meeting of these two? The Earth Plane! And so the Cradle would indicate an area sprinkled with newly sponsored souls to emerge with those of the sprinkling of Terra souls. Are we defined?

Response: "I understand."

BRAZIL

Now that you understand the history, do you not see the importance of this? We shall look at what you refer to as a jungled area, the Amazon Valley.

Now he stands and his hand is projecting light into all of Brazil.

This area will become a power center for the world. For you see, Dear ones, it will become a Center of Exchange.

He is now showing this area as a financial center of the world.

All forms of bartering and monetary systems will merge into one center. This area will become the base on which your new economic structure will be formed.

Question: What natural resources accommodate this?

While, indeed, this area is highly accessible and easily reached through forms of transportation, it is its habitable climate during the Times of Changes and through the transition and cleansing periods. Many people will see this area as stable.

He indicates that for some reason this area is relatively stable during global changes.

Question: "So just the fact that there will be a culture maintained will create the stable development of economic recovery?"

This is true. I speak to you and we impart the warning that this area is to be honored as a Cradle for we will not allow misuse of this area. We will not allow strategic missile sites. We will not allow the underground bases.

This is to be a cradle and a place to nurture. Beyond what you understand as the mining capability, there is an abundance of silver, gold, plutonium, galacia, manganese, and rita contained within this area. These minerals come to the forefront and bring their ancient knowledge of whence they came.

Remember, precious ones, as these mineral substances have densified to the physical level, they have been brought forth for the uplifting miracle of healing. Peace and prosperity reign in the free exchange within this area. To the East we open a harbor as a portal of safety from the mouth of this river, and a vee is cut. For should not such a Cradle, with such nurturing abundant energy, be open to receive the gifts? Are we defined?

Response: "Yes."

I have imparted much information today. And we ask for you to disseminate it. Call upon me again to complete our work. I bless the Earth Plane. I bless the Earth Planet. I AM Archais!

RIO DE JANEIRO

Saint Germain comes forward.

Dear hearts, we bless and thank this radiant angel of light for bringing forth much needed material for you to understand the nature of this area. And now I would like to impart one detail to you of changes within the South American continent, in the area of Rio de Janeiro as you call it. I would like to impart the knowledge of high earthquake activity. The shifting of the ground sets a divide which will run for 485 kilometers. Do you see this and perceive this, Dear ones?

Response: "Yes."

And now, through this wondrous canal, will be created another port of accessibility. Do you have questions?

Response: "No, not on this. We do have the map ready for names. Please define the geographical area to me and we shall look at the names. If you could precipitate it to check it out to give the names or any other information."

THE GOLDEN CITIES OF CENTRAL AMERICA

It is time for the insertion of the Four Pillars. From the center of Mexico, a Vortex area, MARNERO. And extending directly south from the islands which you have labeled Bridge, to that into the ocean waters and touching briefly to the coast of the South American land, I give you this name, CROTESE. The third, JEHOA, will emerge on the new lands to rise. The fourth, ASONEA.

There is a large table and on it he has laid down four maps. The fifth one is a rather big map.

Greetings chelas. Do you see the work laid before you? Do you see what you signed the agreement to complete? I am here for your assistance today, and would like to present this information to you to awaken you to your purpose. Do I have your permission?

Response: "Yes."

He now holds up the first Map, which is the I AM America map and indicates that it is complete.

THE SPIRITUAL VIBRATION OF THE I AM AMERICA MAPS

Completion. This was the first phase of your work, and the completion of many lessons of Mastery and initiation. The second map is the Heart/Cradle map, which outlines Central America or Heartlands and the Cradle, South America. This is also to be known as the Motherland Map. The third is a map of which you consider to be the Eastern Civilizations of the planet. This is a map of rebirth and regeneration to be called the Greening Map. The fourth map is showing Europe and Africa, what you have considered to be your western cultures, a pathway called the Map of Exchanges. They all carry a similar vibration.

Do you not see, Dear ones, the series of events? Do you not see four maps which cover this planet? Four maps which bring completion to the end of this age and the period of transition.

Now, let us discuss the fifth map, which represents the movement to the Fifth Dimension. The map of the Galactic Web, for you will lay the groundwork in completion of the four lower maps. See, Dear ones, as we work on Vortex areas we are able to more readily access the information for the Galactic Web. The four maps comprise the fifth.

Response: "Yes."

I'm asking him, myself, about the Ring Map.

This information is from Ancient Druidic cultures and is information to be imparted from Beloved Kuthumi. It is the map of Elemental Life Force for your planet. What formerly served in the many ringed circle is now known as the Galactic Web. Do you understand?

Response: "Yes."

And so, Dear ones, do you have complete focus? Do you see this work?

Response: "Yes."

ACCEPT THE GIFT

There is a manner and an order in which we dispense information. It is not randomly given as you may perceive. We prefer our candidates to be acquainted, and with a level of initiation. But, as it is in the physical, it is the same within the spiritual worlds. We work with what we have, and so you have been presented with an opportunity to work with another member. Do you not see, Dear ones, it is not exactly as you would want it. But you must work with what you have. Many times, if we had waited for another to sincerely open the doors, and if we have waited for the perfect opportunity, the perfect human being, (which by the way we've yet to see), we would have never worked. Do you understand?

Response: "Yes, I do. We each have our talents, our abilities. I can see where his input would greatly speed things up and make it more efficient."

It is hard for you to accept opportunity, for you deal with the lower nature constantly checking you, balancing you, questioning you, doubting you. But keep your focus, Dear ones, and work with opportunity. There is the saying that the universe will continually supply and you are to experience universal principle.

Supply to you has been another member, your Brother. Do not turn your back upon the work he offers to impart, or squabble over money, or squabble over rights, or squabble over whose work this is. It is your work together, and I emphasize to you, yours. It does not belong to one more than it belongs to the other. But we do emphasize orderliness, which is not speaking of control. We are speaking of an order of dispensation. For the dispensing of the information requires a level of responsibility and the dispensing has been placed within your hands. Do not doubt this. We have given this to you, because we have seen the level at which you perform.

It is by no mistake that this map of America, first stage, has gone to forty-four states. And so it is with the second phase of the Motherland Map. Accept this free gift given to you, your Brother who walks and takes your hand. See him as your sibling, the same as yourself. But understand the responsibility for your role as well. Do you have questions?

Question: "How do you want this organized?"

The organization is already accomplished. For you see, Dear ones, that nothing happens through chance but through choice and a Divine Plan. You must trust the organization as it is. Do you not see that you had offered yourself to this project before your Brother entered your life? Isn't it a choice that he has come to you and that he has come to offer his gift? Ask him and remind him, is this a gift? Is this what you bring to us, your gift? Do you understand? There may be a time for remuneration. But make clear the understanding, if he is to give a gift. And now I turn the floor over to Beloved Sananda who would like to give a message.

Salutations and Greetings to those upon the Earth Plane and Planet. I embrace you with my heart and project to you love and again beg of you to give up indifference. Give up the fear of deception. I beg of you to let go of this lower energy. Fear, hate, mistrust, and doubt. Do you not understand this project is being given to you? It is your free gift. Do we squabble over a gift? Do you not see, Dear hearts, that the gift is to be extended? You have indeed a period of two years to dispense this gift and all you see is much work. Is not another gift now given to you? I beg of you to dispense our gift. Share our gift in the form in which it comes and then look beyond the form, beyond its content and experience the gift. Are you clear, Dear one?

Response: "Yes, this will help a great deal."

We are in a Time of Transition. We perceive timelessness, but you are under the restriction of time. The minutes and seconds click and the awakening is at hand. The time has come for man to receive the gift. Extend our gift! I AM yours in eternal love.

Now he's stepping aside. Saint Germain comes forward.

Dear ones, do you see the series of events we have placed before you? As we again make the agreement, I urge you to have an agreement with those who work with you on these intimate levels. For remember, in the human form, what is communicated verbally is often misunderstood. This is your Brother, an extension of universal love. Remember, I have given you the discourse on agreement. Is this not the proper time to apply it?

He stands back, waiting for our response.

Response: "Yes, we understand."

And so, Dear ones, are we in agreement?

Response: "Yes."

And with most joy, we would like to complete this map of the Cradle, the Motherland. And most graciously impart it to you.

CHAPTER TWENTY
with Saint Germain, Mother Mary,
and Peter the Everlasting

Everno

*"What is eternal and everlasting is as
simple as the scent of a fragrant flower."*
- PETER THE EVERLASTING

Dear chelas, salutations and greetings! We are most excited for the work that you continue to bring forth upon the Earth Plane and Planet at this time, and I bring with me my Beloved Mother as she had sponsored me! For you see, Dear ones, this area which you work upon is the area which she now sponsors. In previous discourse, you were introduced to the guiding angel; now we give you the guiding force which, through human embodiment, has felt the Earth Planet.

We have given you a discourse on the work of angels. Angels are those which have never experienced physical embodiment and, consequently, never bonded with the Earth. Yet their bond is that of Service to the Earth Plane, to what is known as the human. Now I introduce the sponsor of this Motherland. She brings you love, through her wisdom and courage. May I introduce her to you?

Response: "Please."

MOTHER MARY

I bring you my greetings from the heart of the womb which is the birthplace of the Christ, the love energy which has been conceptualized within the soul and extended from the heart of Mother-Father Creation, Alpha-Omega. Dear ones, my love is everlasting to you and to the planet. Dear ones, I am here to impart my gift. Will you accept?

Response: "Yes, gladly."

Love is an eternal flame, a flame which has burned through eons. It is a flame which leaps from one heart to the next. It is a conductive energy force, and from my heart this flame leaps to you.

You have understood this as the Pink Ray and thus it has been imparted to you. Now, you must indeed include Blue Ray energy, truth. For this is a dispensation of the Violet Flame! We move to understand Forgiveness, Mercy, and Compassion; for within this Motherland, this map information will express the forgiving force of nature. For this land sponsored many of the first embodiments of Earth Plane entities and souls. It is through their unwillingness to cooperate among one another that catastrophe occurs. Yet, it was not an unwillingness of cooperation among those of the Earth Planet sponsored in embodiment. And so you come together again to offer Forgiveness to one another, and the mother offers hers as well.

She extends her hands and light streams! One streams pink, the other stream is blue. They come together in a Violet Ray.

Please direct your questions towards me for your assistance.

Question: "The Golden Cities, just after the changes stop, and before the new lands are formed 200 years from now, I'm looking for their locations. One will be in the Mexico mainland, the other one in the Yucatan area which is now Yucatan?"

That is incorrect. There is one in the central part of Mexico. The second is east of the Yucatan, a tip of this area extending to the Florida coastline.

Question: "It would be in the middle of Cuba?"

It is approximate. The apex is located in this area.

Question: "Then the other one, where the tall mountains form, is there an island or will it form on the tip of the mainland?"

Dear one, this is an apex whose focus is on the land to rise; however, the availability of its entrance is upon the existing land.

She's taking my hand and showing me where this is.

We take a short break and continue.

Greetings chelas. We open the portal for communication and remind you that we must ask, for this is the creation of agreement.

Response: "Yes. you have permission. We are looking for more of the names in the Heartland area, the area of the bridge."

A DIMENSION BEYOND CAUSE AND EFFECT

Walk with me to the garden. We have concepts to discuss to continue this work. May I bring with us and introduce you to Peter for he will introduce to you the key.

He's walking with us to this garden. Saint Germain, Peter, and I are walking down a path of golden light. The path gleams like gold. We are all holding hands.

Question: "Is this Peter one of the disciples?"

You have known me as such, but I say to you, I AM Peter the Everlasting. My work is holding the key.

We stop in the garden, surrounded by flowers. We all sit.

Sit and observe amongst this garden for I know the garden well. Do you see, Dear hearts, what is eternal and everlasting is but as simple as the scent of a fragrant flower? You look at this map to decipher what is everlasting and yet simple.

He writes the word, EVERNO.

CUBA

Everno is the word I wish you to become acquainted with. Everno is the word which symbolizes what is unchanged. This concept is difficult for human consciousness to grasp, for change is as constant as the weather in your dimension. In the other realms, what is unchanged, we call Everno. This is where we sit, in this Garden of Everno.

He now places the word "Everno" on the Island of Cuba.

Everno Island. For you see, this is an island which has experienced change, change, change! And where does this change lead but to what becomes changeless. Dear ones, you have inquired who I am. From the past I tell you, I came as Cortez to this region. And yet, this island is now renamed and reclaimed as Everno; for you see, this is my role, to bring it to alignment. As you have met, discussed, and discoursed with Beloved Mary; I shall discuss my work as holder of the key. I am here to assist you in interpretation and gladly open the floor for your questions.

Question: "By the key, I'm assuming the names?"

Names represent cubits, measurements, and patterns.

Question: "I am fascinated by the island with the five lakes in the center of the Sea of Mirrors. What is the name associated with it?"

Barbond.

He is now speaking in a language I don't understand. I'll interpret as best as I can.

Question: "Does this island have any special energies or significance?"

THE TRINITY OF LOVE, WISDOM, AND POWER

You see, this island arises in the center of the heart. Inside this island is indeed a flame, or a plume, as you would call it. A time will come when this plume will surround the island as a dance of color or a dance of the Rays. And so this ancient name, Barbond, means the dancing island, to be known as an island of dancing flame!

Bond with one another. For to do so, one first searches for power. Two then emerge with love and wisdom. Bond with one another. For to do so, one then searches to find love. Two emerge with wisdom and power. Bond. One goes within to find wisdom and two emerge to find love and power. These qualities are the attributes of this island. It is a place to touch, and go within the true heart. And what a joy this is! What a dance of life it becomes! The dancing island becomes the dance of the flame!

A TIMELESS HEART

Look up with me to the stars. Can you count them? They are endless and timeless. You begin to count six, twelve, twenty-four and so on. These stars, count them to become your companions, your watches, your keepers. For you recognize their light and they recognize you. Everno! I say to you, experience eternity. For in the Times of Changes, few will believe. In a world which rapidly changes in front of your eyes would you not, too, doubt the existence of something which could not be changed? I have come to give you the key. Please, now, direct your questions.

Question: "Are you making a reference to going within the heart, or going within our soul in meditations to a place of timelessness?"

Go within the heart, and understand through love, wisdom, and power that universal law and principle brings the timeless, changeless, energy force! This concept seems foreign, and yet is crucial!

Question: "Can you tell me about the mountain range to the East?"

The Silver Crystal Mountains. These four mountain peaks are to be named, Pillar Peaks. They represent the four pillars.

CHAPTER TWENTY-ONE
with Saint Germain, Mother Mary,
El Morya, and Kuan Yin

Bay of the Golden Sun

"I come to serve and extend love to this Earth."
- KUAN YIN

Welcome, Beloved chelas. Let us finish the greater work. Be present with us to accompany us on this mission. We bring with us Beloved Mary, she who holds the cradle. Beloved El Morya, who continues to hold the focus for wisdom; Kuan Yin, whose Divine Compassion is the extension of the loving heart of God.

Now we're walking down a hallway together. We enter the workroom. At the back, three maps are pinned up. The Heartland Map is on the table.

THE GULF OF MEXICO

Welcome, Dear ones. It is an honor to continue this work with you. As you see, we are in a final stage of refinement. Our Vortex areas are in place; coastlines and lake lines in place. The remaining structures to be added are certain strategic points. Primarily, what you have called the Gulf of Mexico we would like to rename the Bay of the Golden Sun. For you see, it was the home of the culture that worshipped the sun, called the Second Race. Its waters now embrace and lap the land from where this Star seed sprang! Her waters celebrate the sun, and divinely inspire! Its light and radiant heat source will shed into our lives, for upon her waters will be an intense magnification of the sun energy. This represents the radiating heart of Alpha and Omega.

A voice begins to speak!

I bring you this message, Dear children of the Earth, from the Heart of the Mother-Father, Alpha and Omega. From this day, the light of the Golden Sun will be greatly intensified in to the heart of Terra. This light of great intensity is the joy of experiencing enlightenment! For this is the focus of this area, joy, absolute joy!

Saint Germain speaks.

Dear ones, excuse the interruption, for that message has come from a hierarchy which exists above me and I have extended to you. We know that at this time, you do not understand the realms which work above us; but, on occasion, you will have the opportunity to experience their radiance. Are there any questions?

Question: "Kuan Yin had made a reference at one point that led me to believe that there would be fresh water on both sides of the Yucatan. Is the Bay of the Golden Sun also a fresh water?"

We will turn the floor over and you may direct your question directly to her.

GOLDEN WATER AND GLACIAL FLOWS

My Beloved Brother and Sister, I am most happy to answer this question. For you see, Dear ones, the flow of glaciers and fresh water lakes and rivers will extremely affect the chemical balance of the waters in what you know as the Gulf of Mexico, soon to become this Great Bay of Golden Light. For, you see, a certain structure will occur in the water itself. The molecular structure of this water will closely resemble the molecular structure of gold. Many will see in her waters a flickering of the substance itself, as a liquified type of gold. A golden sheen will spread across the waters. Some will explain this as a mineral balance in the water, but truly I say to you, it is the gift from the heart of Alpha and Omega, that of vibrant joy, the joy of life!

If you were to look up the crystalline structure of gold, you would get an exact proportion for the waters in this area. It is the balance of sodium, hydrogen, and oxygen. Not only will this promote the great sheen upon the water, but allow for new vegetation, and, in some cases, new animal life to spring from these waters. Many new species will develop here. I am delighted that this gift has been given to the

Earth Planet Terra. This is a playground of waters! Have I sufficiently answered your request?

Question: "It will be of salt water content but much less than our oceans are in the present?"

Much less. For you see, Dear one, you have the glacier flows.

Question: "So there will be the high mountains and the glaciers in the Yucatan area here?"

You have ice sheets which will be coming down from the North combined with wind patterns coming from the East. The extreme temperature combined with the ice sheeting will promote melting for fresh water supplies. Combined with that, as you know, the ocean current and shifting of earth plates creates a natural flow into this Golden Bay.

Question: "The Bay of the Golden Sun in the central states, is referenced as the gift from the Central Sun?"

This is indeed the gift from the Central Sun, a gift from Alpha/Omega to the Motherland, a place of joy!

Question: "The present area of the Yucatan we have shown as an island. Is that a flat semi-marshy area or is it high mountains?"

It is a peninsula, a peninsula not a marsh, a peninsula that is pastoral.

Response: "Okay."

But you are correct in assuming its lowland elevation. Much of this area will be used in the future for the production of vegetables.

Response: "Okay. I am trying to perceive where the mountains and the glacier movements will end, as they come around from the East towards the Vortex area."

My Dear ones, they come, write this down, 70 degrees down latitude.

Response: "Okay."

84.6 kilometers off the coastline of northern Florida.

ICE SHEETS

She now shows the break-up of the ice which covers New England slipping off, going out, traveling down some sort of ocean current coming off the coastline, 84.6 kilometers from Florida. There are even larger amounts coming down from Europe. These ice sheets are massive.

Question: "So we will be having another strong glacier period in the 200 years after the changes?"

My dear, you must understand the compaction of time and understand this as a Time of Transition and Cleansing. All earth elements will be experienced, for they, too, must undertake the transition and cleanse. Wondrous things are to happen upon the planet Terra at this time, and the wonders presented to your eyes are ones over which science will exclaim! You will have complete glacier ice caps which will form in a matter of hours and disseminate in days. This has to do with the tears within the atmosphere pinpointed directly to areas of Europe as you know them now. But we will save this information for a later date and further study what is within the grasp of your understanding. Understand the movement of ice and the fact that ice does indeed melt. My Dear ones, may I assist you further?

Question: "Okay, from what you were just telling me, I'm seeing the ice flow coming down along the East Coast forming the mountains in the area of Cuba, that range in there. Then the other range that will be formed on the East side will be coming up from the sea bed?"

This is all a part of the transitional shift into the Golden Age. This is an Age of Cooperation and again the mountains which extend through the United States carry throughout into the Heartland area of the Motherland.

Response: "Right."

THE AMETHYST CITY

The Amethyst City is the portal. The Amethyst City is in Cuba, as it exists now. Beloved, the radiation from the Amethyst City serves as a portal to those who seek the Lake of Mirrors. Do you see this natural progression? First the cleansing of the heart, and great shedding of water. Then this clean heart expands across the great lake of the Golden Sun, expressing joy. And then onward to the Lake of Mirrors and this joy is now held by the cellular memory. It delights my soul that this gift has been offered. And now, my Dears, I turn the floor to she who holds the cradle, Beloved Mary.

> I AM the Way.
> I AM the Resurrection and the Light.
> I AM the Light, the Light of the Heart.

My Dear ones, I send my blessings and my prayers to you, and ask of you to raise you radiance to me. FOR I AM a loving mother and I enfold you in my love and care. I bless this work that you are about to impart. While, indeed, my focus is the cradle, I AM a mother as well! I would like to give you the name of the island South from Resurrection. This is an island which serves as a focus for the energy of pure intent, the Immaculate Conception. So we will name this island which combines two words into one: Creator and Conception, Conceptor Island!

She mentions that they originally had planned to name the island Madonna but felt, for the New Age, that it should have a name all cultural backgrounds would understand. She withdraws, holding a lighted candle close to her heart.

Question: "What about the pyramid area?"

El Morya is stepping forward.

THE RISE OF THE WISDOM SCHOOLS OF ASCENSION

That which arises is the wisdom schools, which explain the mysteries of the ages. Through this comes the knowledge which will raise the Sixth Race to the science of Ascension. For this is the knowledge which they have not had a chance to experience as the Fifth Race prepared to leave. Do you not see, Dear ones, it is this Fifth Race which brought forth the school of wisdom to uncloak these ancient mysteries. There are those within the Sixth Race who have not had the opportunity to pattern their minds to experience these truths. I am here to give you specific information, if you please. However, I am not allowed to impart without your full cooperation and agreement.

Response: "This you have."

And now, Dear ones, for your assistance I open the floor.

Question: "What will be the area where the pyramid rises? What will this be called and what are its characteristics?"

It is close to that area which you had indicated in the Indies and Bahama area.

He now writes the numbers, 48 Southeast.

Question: "It's 408 kilometers Southeast of where I have it now?"

408 kilometers Southeast from the existing tip of Florida.

Response: "Okay, that's close."

In the beginning, as the rising of the lands commences, a series of volcanic activities occurs as Beloved Kuthumi activates the Ring of Fire. And from this, the creative forces bring forth a new island, an island to herald the arising of that of what you have known as Atlantis. This island shall be named the Star Island, as the first born star! And in a period no less than twenty years, a section of the land will begin to emerge. This time comes after the melting of ice.

CHAPTER TWENTY-TWO
with Saint Germain, Sananda,
Mother Mary, Kuan Yin, and Paul

Open Doors

*"It is you, through God, who has sculpted
and determined your destiny."*
- SAINT GERMAIN

PERSONAL CHOICES SCULPT YOUR DESTINY

Greetings Dear ones, I bring to you this message of thanks and praise as your work continues in the physical plane. This is a Time of Choice, a time which has been brought to you to choose your path. All paths lead to ONE as you well know, and yet there is the human factor of free will and free choice. When we speak of the will and its alignment to the God source, we then begin to see and experience the opening of doors, potentials, side roads. And so the doors open and you ask, "Is this the Will of God?" God truly opens these doors for you; then it is up to you to walk through them. God judges not your past, but allows you to step presently into a future. Do you see this great gift of the will, free choice, and responsibility?

Have you not seen through the course of this work the many doors which are opened and the many which are closed? God opens the doors. You choose the door you wish to walk through. This is the cooperative and complementing force that exists between mankind and God. You may say, well, God is controlling me by presenting only these open doors and not the one that I wish to have. This is not so, Dear hearts. As you walk through the first door of your choice, it determines the next series of doors to be opened. Do you not see how you are creative with your choices? You see yourself as babes, yet it is you, through God, who has sculpted and determined your destiny.

Things do not happen by chance. They happen by choice in Divine Order. There will be more choices in your work. Many are brought to work of this nature, but remain focused, Dear ones, and remain true to yourself, the mighty I AM Presence. I have taken much time and wish to turn the floor over to Beloved Sananda.

My Brother and Sister, I AM come this day to complete a phase of our work. I am here with Beloved Mary, Beloved Kuan Yin, and Beloved Paul. I would like to first open the floor for questions on completion of the Central American area and then would like to travel with you down the coast of South America.

Response: "We have no questions on the Central area."

Beloveds, do you recall when I placed the dove upon the first map? This I placed as a request for tranquility and peace to come to the United States. It is the same dove that I ask you to carry throughout your work. Tranquility, harmony, peace, are these not attributes which we all seek? I ask you to recall the dove, its purpose and meaning. We have placed it through choice upon this map and it is no mistake. Remember, this is the focus of your being. As Beloved Saint Germain has spoken of the open doors, you must say to yourself, is this tranquil, is this in harmony, is this in peace? That is the key to the Divine Will. If there is fear, there is no love. If there is resentment, there is no harmony. See and recognize this in the action of choice.

Response: "Yes, we're keeping a dove on all our printed materials. Thank you for the reminder of its symbology."

THE GOLDEN CITIES OF SOUTH AMERICA

And now we travel on to the coastline.

Sananda and I hold hands, and together look down at South America. First we stand at a delta area in the northern tip, then travel inland.

This Vortex area is named Andeo.

Question: "Is it in Peru?"

Yes.

He now takes me to another Vortex in the center of Brazil.

This is the Vortex, Braham.

Then we travel South, towards the end of South America.

This is named Tehekoa.

THE CHRISTED LEADERS OF THE NEW TIMES

Beloveds, I have revealed to you the location of the seven Vortices. As you see, there are the four pillars in the central area, and the three Sisters which accompany these pillars in South America. They symbolize the Seventh Root Race. The Seventh are the Christed beings who are emerging at this time, those who are the leaders of the Golden Age. These beings are coming specifically from seven planets! The majority are indeed incarnating in this area; however, there are many scattered across the planet and, for one choice or another, find compatibility with those who are their co-sponsors. As we have revealed these Vortex areas to you, we should also assign attributes. It is time for me to choose!

He sits down with a pen and the map.

Question: "What are the attributes of these Vortices?"

ANDEO, Consistency. TEHEKOA, Devotion. BRAHAM, The Nuturer. MARNERO, Virtue.

CHAPTER TWENTY-THREE
with Saint Germain, Sananda, and Kuan Yin

White Dove

"Do not forget the timeliness of these events. Each is orderd as you are ordered. Each is created as you are created."
- PAUL

LOVE IS AN ACTION

Beloved Sananda speaks.

I come to you in love and appreciation of your work and send this message to you. Follow your heart at all times. Follow your heart, for the work that you do is, indeed, an extension of yourself. There are times we speak of the mind through which the will functions. And then there is the broader based will, which is the will of cosmic Service. Follow your hearts, Dear ones, to achieve the most appropriate benefit from this work. Be led and guided by your heart.

We have spoken of love as energy, and so you have experienced the energy. It is now time to use this energy in all that you do. Listen, look, and receive. I have come to offer you my support and beg of you to call to me in matters of understanding love. This is an energy which must continue to flow, for it is on the wave length of this energy that we perform our work with you. It is important to keep this flowing. Yes, this is a form of cooperation. But it is the synthesis or end result, as you call it, of cooperation. It is love.

We have repeatedly said that all is love. And we are most happy to serve you through love. And it is our hope that you experience it in greater measure in your life at all times. Do not hesitate to call to us. See us too, as a safe harbor, for our time in the physical was spent with purpose. Follow your heart, Dear ones, and you are released to universal Oneness.

He's stepping back. Saint Germain is coming forward.

It is with expedient measure, my Dear ones, that I introduce to you, Beloved Kuan Yin.

I greet you with the compassion of my heart and being and release this message to mankind.

> The winds begin to blow.
> The Four Pillars are to shake.
> The seed has been sown.

Then she's saying the vase is to break.

Question: "This is the second time we've had reference to the wind coming very soon. Could you be more specific on the event?"

My Dear ones, I am not allowed to give you a date, but I am allowed to warn you.

Saint Germain speaks.

My Dear ones, take light of Prophecy! While brought in sternness, it is brought for your upliftment.

And now I see that you have brought the map of the Motherland. And I will facilitate directing the details for expedient measures. Please direct your questions, Dear one.

Question: "What is the name of the island on the West coast?"

White Dove. Its shape resembles that of the wing of a dove.

Question: "Is there a name for the bay by Rio De Janeiro?"

Bay of Continuity.

Question: "What about the tip that is broken up into islands? Does this area have a name?"

There is a discussion.

Regeneration Islands.

Question: "Any cities that will be significant?"

Brasilia will become known as the Center City. Rio De Janeiro becomes known as the City of the Dancing Light.

Question: "Is there a city by the Bay of Hope?"

More discussion.

The Charitable City.

Question: "Before I forget, what are the attributes for the Vortex South of Florida? Asonea."

Regeneration.

WHITE DOVE ISLAND

Question: "Thank you. I'm drawn toward the White Dove Island. What significance does that area have?"

It is a part of the continent of Atlantis which rises, and which served as the birth place of the Red Race. The white dove symbolizes the silver cord in Red Race history. For the white dove is the symbol of the free flowing energy exchange between the God Source and humanity. Does this properly explain?

Response: "Yes."

It is an emergence of land which will be seen approximately 2030 A.D.

There is more discussion. Two names for rivers, River From the Source and The Nurturing River. They wish for you to put these names in.

Okay.

There is still discussion over another name. River of Strength, the name they've chosen.

Dear hearts, if we are through with the question period, I would like to further instruct you on use of the Violet Flame activity at this time. It is important that you use the Violet Flame no less than three times per day. Do you understand?

Response: "Yes."

I AM lovingly yours!

CHAPTER TWENTY-FOUR
Saint Germain and Sananda
introduce the Twelve Jurisdictions

Expansive Completion

"I am not allowed to infringe upon your free will, Dear one. However, I am for your assistance."
- SANANDA

COMPLETION ENGENDERS AN EXPANSIVE BEGINNING

Greetings Beloved Saint Germain.

Welcome my Beloved chela. I step forth on the mantle of consciousness that comes forth on the Seventh Ray, what is the Violet Transmuting Flame of Mercy and Forgiveness. I am here to complete our work. What I have started is what I have come to complete. You see Dear ones, within your density and world there are many who step forward to start, but there are few who have the initiative to complete.

Completeness, in itself, sets forth the energetic pattern to perpetuate. Creation comes forth not only on what is started but also on what has been completed. For you see, the rhythm comes forth and is sealed and is held within the consciousness. Dear one, when we have been using Violet Flame, do you not seal this rhythm and pattern within your heart? And so we ask that all that you do, to come forth as complete, to seal it, to set it into motion. For you see it is a pattern which has been brought forth through duplication. And as you seal this, the energetic pattern comes forth and you are truly ready for the expansion. For what moves forth to completion is then ready to expand. Do you understand?

Question: "Yes, please continue."

I have come forth with this information this morning for you Dear one. For you see there have been many who are interested within the work, but the energetic pattern is that you have not completed. It is important that you come forth to complete these patterns, to set them forth for expansion. You see, we have set a pattern in motion, a pattern that another may come upon, to also set in motion. Do you understand what I mean by crucial?

Response: "Yes."

And so we ask for you Dear one, to step forward to be that complete force.

Question: "I am most willing."

THE RHYTHMIC, CREATIVE WAVE

For you see, what comes forth to complete is what sets the seal and sets the pattern of duplication, the creative wave which is built upon to expand. Do you see how a plan can be set in motion and diverted and the final outcome is totally incompatible with the foundation?

Question: "Very easily."

And this is what has been set forth.

Question: "Please outline what you desire for me to complete."

Number One, the priority as set forth from Beloved Brother Sananda, that of the World Map. To set this into completion would seal this work and only what would step forward from that point is what would expand to support this work.

Number Two, I ask that the energetic work be complete. For in understanding such, you will understand the products that have been brought forth, the technology to aid and assist mankind during planetary transition and lead mankind into the period of Grace.

Do you see how these three have been set forth for the projects at hand?

Question: "Yes, please continue."

Dear One, it is important that you understand what comes forth as rhythm. For in nature, all things work with a rhythm and an orderliness. As you have been selected to complete this work, there are indeed those who will capitalize or should we say, ride the wave, the creative wave and pattern you have set forth, the rhythm.

Question: "Yes, I understand that."

And so Dear One, this is the work that we have set forth as a creative wave, a rhythm as you would say.

Question: "Now, may I ask one question?"

Proceed.

Question: "It is important to me that I do not interrupt when you are bringing forth information. May I question everything at the end of your discourse? May we have that as the rhythm?"

We may do this; however, there are times, in your silence, I hear your questions.

Question: "The questions in my heart that I don't verbalize?"

And so I offer the break, for you to relay these to me. I am not allowed to infringe upon your free will, Dear one. However, I am for your assistance.

Question: "It is just most important to me that my questions remain focused upon what it is that you are bringing forth."

Dear One, whatever form will work, we are willing to do. Our Beloved Brother Sananda is here for your assistance.

Question: "What is it that you wish to bring forth?"

LOVE ONE ANOTHER

Greetings my Beloved Brother and Sister. I AM Sananda, and I step forth to remind you of the work that you have brought to this plane and planet during transition. Do you remember Dear ones as we gathered together as a family to sup and to share, before we came to this planet?

And we vowed to one another at that time above all things, what would we do? To love one another and to bring forth harmony. There is discord in your family, Dear one. However, we realize the free will that has come forth. We ask that you continue this work in harmony.

Question: "Yes, that would be most acceptable to me. How do we achieve this harmony?"

As simply stated, love one another.

Question: "I understand. Bring forth what you now desire."

I AM the Harmony of God. I AM the Creator. Above all, we request harmony and love to allow the creative wave to expand. It is discipline, motivation, and desire that sets forth a creative wave in duplication. It is harmony and love that allows it to expand. Dear one, we ask that you complete this project within the next few months.

Question: "The project is just the maps?"

This Map of World Changes that I give to you.

Question: "What form do you consider completion?"

We would like to see a completed product to be dispensed throughout the third density plane.

Question: "Do you wish this to be in book form, as an atlas?"

We would prefer such; however, given the time constraints, whatever form you deem necessary.

Question: "Could we complete a fold out map, and then continue with the atlas? With the discourses in the atlas book?"

Yes. It is important that I give you the Twelve Jurisdictions.

Question: "Prior to the completion of the map?"

Prior to completion.

Response: "Then I accept that, and we will commence today, if you so desire."

CHAPTER TWENTY-FIVE
Sananda presents the First Jurisdiction

Harmony

The Law of Agreement

"All energy, in order to be sustained for creation, must be maintained in balance. Balance is the continuous cycle of Harmony."
- SANANDA

EARTH CHANGES AND THE SPIRITUAL HIERARCHY

Welcome my Beloved Brother and Sister, I AM Sananda. I come forth this day to give you continued discourse on what we call the World Project at this time upon your Earth Plane. Do we have permission to enter your energy fields?

Response: "You most certainly have permission to enter my energy field. And I'm sure Lori would give her permission."

Dear ones, we have come forth to offer this project to you, the world changes to occur upon the Earth Plane and Planet. We also have come to bring you discourse or lesson. For you see, this project was originated through Beloved Sanat Kumara many eons ago and this is its completion; for he has expanded on the laws of the cosmos as a creative pattern.

There are, as you understand, several reasons for what has come forth. Change is a continual process, and it is most important that humankind understand that change is the pathway whereby growth is achieved. This is, indeed, the seventh time that the Earth will go through what you call a shift, a shift not only of the poles themselves but of the electromagnetic currents that run through her energy fields.

This shift in energy will occur from her sixth to her seventh body, preparing humankind to enter into what is called the Fourth Dimension. Third Dimensional beings are being prepared to enter into a Fourth Dimension awareness.

As I have stated before, there are Twelve Jurisdictions to accompany this work. The theme of Earth Changes is to be understood in its entire context. I shall recognize those who have helped tirelessly with this effort and work:

Beloved Saint Germain, Sponsor of the Americas.

Beloved Mary, Keeper of what is the Cradleland, also known as South America.

Beloved Kuan Yin, who has stepped forth to sponsor the Asian Continent.

Beloved El Morya, whose directive focus is shared in America and in Europe.

Beloved Kuthumi, who has generously given his light to America and also holds the channel and light for Africa.

There are many more to follow and many more will come forth, many, too numerous to mention. There is indeed, Beloved Nada, who holds her radiance and presence within England. There is also Beloved Paul, who comes to set the seal of his radiance and brilliance in the Central American areas. And, most assuredly, the Seven Beloved Archangels shed their Rays on the entire planet. And who stands at the North and South poles? Beloved Archangel Michael. And who is that who sheds the Ray of Golden Radiance around the equator and surrounds the planet in eternal love, but Archangel Chamuel.

So you see, Dear one, this is a method of cooperation and we work in Harmony, which is, indeed, the topic of our first Jurisdiction, Harmony.

WE ARE ALL IN THIS TOGETHER

Beloveds, you have been brought here to create. Not only are you creative beings, but you must learn to create in full cooperation with one another. You are, at times, like small children in a sandbox, designing your castle. Each of you has the same sand, the same amount of water, and yet, as one designs the building that is his, there is always someone who comes forth to throw sand or to destroy what his Brother or Sister has made. So each person then rebuilds again. It is time for you to let this go! It is time for you to work in co-operation and Harmony! Together, for you are in this truly together. Not only have you shared genetic code, you are on this planet as ONE body of light. It is time for you to come forth and cooperate.

HARMONY MAINTAINS BALANCE

Harmony comes forth for the blending of creative waves. Harmony comes forth when all has achieved balance. We have spoken of alignment and spoken of balance. Alignment must precede balance. Balance is, indeed, the maintenance of alignment. You have yet to achieve this upon your planet. There have, indeed, been times when she has become aligned, but the maintenance of alignment is balance, and this is yet to be achieved. We speak of the directive force within the will itself. For you see, Dear one, mankind has long forgotten that will is to be directed only through love, not through wisdom. Wisdom is the application. But we speak now of direction.

What is the directive force? The directive force of the will is love. To understand this is to become aligned. And to maintain this universal law is to achieve balance. The maintenance of balance, Dear ones, is the nature of our project. Not only is your planet misaligned, it is far from balanced. Earth Changes have been brought forth to provide the creative space and pattern for alignment. You, as human beings, have long understood that all energy, in order to be sustained for creation, must be maintained in balance. To draw from the well of creativity, to drink of its waters, the source must be replenished. And how does the source replenish? Through balance, Dear ones.

Question: "Balance is the continuous cycle?"

It is the continuous cycle known as Harmony.

And so upon your planet, do you not see the imbalance, the misalignment, and how this has come to be? Each continent is to become aligned. Ascended Beings have come forth to sponsor, to not only keep the alignment, but to hold a focus for maintenance. That is why we are dispensing the information which you know as the energetic bodies of perfection. Man has long known that he was a body of light, but he has refused to recognize this within himself. And now this must be recognized for truly he must be responsible for what he has created.

So you see, Dear ones, you enter into the misappropriation of energy which allows a non-creative force to exist. You have referred to this as a black hole. And eventually, yes, you pull out of this hole into another dimension of creation. It is no mystery to the cosmos that the Earth, through her inhabitants, has created a pattern, a pattern of imbalance, a pattern of disharmony, and a pattern of misalignment. We have stepped forth as members of the Spiritual Hierarchy of the Great White Brotherhood not to duplicate this pattern. We have decided to expand it!

If you are to be a creative planet, Dear ones, create in Harmony. If you are to create Harmony, sustain your creation. We are here to assist you, Dear ones. Harmony is your first lesson. I am here, eternally yours. Are you ready for questions?

THE CONSCIOUSNESS OF MINERALS AND CRYSTALS

Question: "Mineral deposits, crystal structures and precious gems, which are crystal structures, they carry the energetic stability of the planet, do they not?"

They have been set forth to hold the creative pattern.

Question: "Then indeed mineral deposits carry consciousness?"

They carry vibration, which, Dear one, is a component of consciousness. Consciousness is a collective vibration.

Question: "Then with reference to the human body and the Earth body comparison, mineral deposits function much the same way as acupuncture meridians do in the human body?"

To the Earth Planet, yes. They also serve as great centers for input and output for the flow of energy, what you have seen on the human body as a chakra point. They assist the planet much as you have understood your nervous system.

Question: "I see. That is the physical mode of how the human nervous system functions. So does the nervous system of the planet function through the mineral deposits?"

FIRST JURISDICTION: HARMONY

THE HARMONIC FLOW OF SOUND

It does indeed. For this is how light travels, on electromagnetic current, which underneath, if you were to isolate this further, is through sound. For sound precedes light.

Question: "As the biblical phrase, 'In the beginning,' there was the word?"

This is true.

Question: "In addition, before the word, there was the sound?"

Sound is the building block that light is built upon.

Question: "So all creation is based upon the first primary building block of sound?"

Sound that carries an electromagnetic field.

Question: "Not all sound carries an electromagnetic field?"

This is true, not all sound is qualified as creative wave.

Question: "So there are certain sound frequencies which work to create, to rebuild, to align, to restructure, to purify and cleanse?"

This is accurate, for do you not have the division of Rays within light?

Question: "Yes. Now if we look at the bodies of water on the planet, which do they function on, the sound or the light, or both?"

You see Dear ones, they function upon a wave and like a wave that comes to the beach, this wave has been predicated by gravitational pull. Beyond the gravitational pull is the energy of light, that streams forth on the electromagnetic current. And what builds the electromagnetic current? Sound. Something as massive as an ocean contains within it the complete harmony and symphony of the Elementals and the Mighty Elohim, those who step forward in Service to the rhythmic, harmonic flow of sound on the electromagnetic wave.

CHAPTER TWENTY-SIX
Sananda presents the Second Jurisdiction

Abundance

The Law of Choice

*"The Creator never infringes upon the path of
abundance of his Brother or Sister,
or take away his choice."*
- SANANDA

Dear ones, welcome. I AM Sananda, and have been brought forth for discourse. For the Time of Planetary Transition draws near, and as this time approaches, it has been requested of us to provide information not only of planetary Earth Change, but information which is designed to enlighten your body, your mind, and your spirit. It is most important that this discourse be set forth with this information of world changes. For it has been recommended by the Planetary Council of Justice that these discourses accompany this Earth Change information. As usual, Dear ones, I must ask for your permission to enter your energy field.

Response: "You most wholeheartedly have my permission to enter my field. You are most welcome my Beloved."

AKASHIC RECORDS

I want to give you a description. He is sitting at a desk. Behind him is a glow of pink and gold light. At the desk he has a huge book that he's offered me. He is turning the pages, and the pages are gold.

Question: "What color are the letters?"

The letters are violet. If there is anything more you'd like to know regarding this scene, now is the time to ask, as he has slowed down purposely so we may observe.

Question: "What kind of desk is this?"

It looks like a piece of stone, much like a piece of green and pink marble.

Question: "And the book has a white cover?"

It has a green cover. Off to his right-hand side Saint Germain is standing, and off to his left-hand side is Archangel Michael.

Question: "This is an important meeting. Where are they?"

Dear ones, we sit at the Chamber of Planetary Justice, which has been brought forth to serve the planet. For you see, each planet within this solar system has a council which oversees its entirety. For the Earth, or Terra, as you have known it, has its guardians and keepers.

Question: "Yes it would. This planetary space is within one of the bodies of the planet, is it not?"

It is contained within the sixth field.

Response: "Thank you."

So Dear ones, may we proceed?

Response: "Please."

He is turning the pages.

ABUNDANCE IS THE NATURAL RESULT OF HARMONY

Abundance.

Throughout the ages on your planet, Abundance is to reign supreme! For this planet was brought forth to be not only the garden, but to be an abundant place. Abundance has long been misrepresented throughout your epochs of history. Abundance has been brought forth to provide choice. Upon your planet you have many paths; this is Abundance. You have many roads and paths to choose; is this not Abundance?

When choice is taken away from mankind, you interfere with the Laws of Abundance. It is the job of the Creator never to infringe upon the path of Abundance of his Brother or Sister, never to take away his choice. We have given the discourse on Harmony which builds to this discourse on Abundance.

I hold in one hand three seeds. And I hold in my other hand fertile earth. I mix them together and they grow abundantly. From another source, comes three seeds. But the soil, barren. Three beautiful seeds, such as those that have just burst forward, yet nothing is produced. The seed is wasted, and the soil, blowing in the wind. What have we done? Mixed vibration, Dear one. Abundance does not come forward when you mix vibration. That is why we give the lesson of Harmony.

In order for Abundance to come forth, you must distinguish vibration, and bring together vibration that mixes harmoniously. Do you understand?

Question: "Yes. I understand that the vibration must have the same focus. Is this correct?"

When a child is brought forth in third density, you have the meeting of the female and the male. A child brought forth only when these two meet in Harmony, as the vibration resonates to the same octave, Creation is then allowed to spring forward. An abundant child is born! A child blessed by health! Have you not seen children who have been born upon your planet who are not healthy? Not abundant in health? The vibration has been altered.

Response: "Yes."

SECOND JURISDICTION: ABUNDANCE

SAME VIBRATION EQUALS AGREEMENT

In Abundance, we have what is called agreement. Agreement is the formation on which Harmony is founded. There is like vibration and there is same vibration. Like vibration will produce results; however, the results are often not abundant. Same vibration brings forth Abundance.

In your world of creation, as you know it, you are at any time able to take the components to make them same vibration. This is done through agreement and Harmony. As any fine musician knows, it is the orchestrated instrument that brings forth the peace of music, music that flows and is soothing to one's ear. This Garden has been created to express Abundance, Abundance for all and for all to choose at all times. One must always view the symphony to hear it playing, to choose what he would like to add. So often we forget this. So we seek more and more, for more to come forth. The Law of Agreement and Harmony is the foundation for the Law of Abundance. Look at any great persons in your history who have achieved Abundance, they have understood the Law of Harmony.

This planet has been brought forth for all to have Harmony, so all may choose to create. Abundance is the bi-product of Harmony. This is a planet originally intended to be abundantly supplied. It is the intent that there should be no 'want.' There should be no *need*. It is the intent that Abundance will flow as a natural course. Abundance Dear ones, is not the hoarding of gold coin. Abundance is a natural flow of choice. When one understands Abundance as a natural flow of choices, one will hear the symphony of the garden.

Abundance is choosing health over disease. Abundance is choosing wisdom over ignorance. Abundance is choosing joy over sorrow. Abundance is choice. Do you hunger, Dear one? Then free yourself. Flow into the world that openly gives and then receives. Questions Dear one?

Question: "Numerous ones. Might I suggest that we continue with this discourse and when it is complete, I will ask questions."

Abundance is the natural law of this planet. It is the end result of the free movement of creative beings. Come forth and live abundantly, Dear ones, Dear children of the Golden Light.

He has turned the page. He is complete. They are closing the book.

I am here to assist you.

Question: "Thank you. Now, I have some confusion about all of this. I understand that Abundance is the basic program for this planet, and that we have all misunderstood that, including myself."

SECOND JURISDICTION: ABUNDANCE

THE DIFFERENCE BETWEEN PROSPERITY AND ABUNDANCE

Abundance and prosperity are two entirely different concepts. Prosperity is the result of right use of the Law of Abundance. Abundance is, indeed, a dance, a dance that allows a-bound-ness!

Question: "Then Abundance, or a-bound-ness, is the openness of a certain frequency of the heart?"

It is indeed so, Dear one. It recognizes the need for choice in all things. It allows for free movement. It allows for options, as you call it. Do you see, in any given situation, where one feels he has no choice? What has then occurred? A blockage. A stoppage of the natural Law of Creativity.

Question: "So then the heart's desire does not flow?"

How could it? For it has been contained and held by another.

Question: "And this containment, more likely, is fear?"

At times you may perceive this as fear. At other times, control is the proper word. Mankind has a tendency to control the dance of a-bound-ness.

Question: "I see, so mankind many times chooses to hold on instead of release and become free and flow?"

Correct, Dear one.

Question: "So this is the time, in these changes, where we let go and we become what we truly desire?"

It is time for you to take your mantle as a creative being, a being blessed with the Creator's individuality, I AM THAT I AM.

Response: "I can understand that it is time; however, in this moment, it is unclear how to do this, other than to just let go and release."

It is important to have flow and movement in all that you do. This is the Law of Abundance. Man has placed the laws of prosperity first. When you place the Law of Prosperity first, you stop the Law of Abundance.

Question: "So the first step is to flow with vibrations that mix harmoniously?"

To exchange and to flow, it is important first to agree and to harmonize your agreement. It is then important to allow free exchange and the flow of Abundance to come forth. The end result is how you prosper.

Question: "Was this why it was so important that we establish a daily schedule? With balance and agreement, we would flow, and then prosperity would follow?"

It is important to harmonize. It is important to agree. Of course, Dear one, two must merge in the Law of Abundance. Do you see, it is an exchange that comes forth! Abundance does not come forth from the work of just one. It always involves the work of two or more. It is the expansive, creative force that you draw upon in your universe.

CHAPTER TWENTY-SEVEN
Sananda presents the Third Jurisdiction

Clarity

The Law of Non-Judgment

*"Light has come forth for clarity.
It has come forth not to judge or discern.
It has come forth simply to BE."*
- SANANDA

Welcome, my Beloved children. I AM Sananda. I have come forth this evening to give you this third discourse to be contained within the upcoming changes, not only for the world, or planet Terra as you know her, but also for the upcoming changes within the plane itself, or what you have known as the collective consciousness of mankind.

Dear ones, as usual, it is most important that I ask permission to come closer to your energy field.

Response: "Dear Beloved Brother, you have our permission, please come closer."

May I enter into your resonance?

Response: "Yes."

Dear one, as we sit preparing for discourse again, I read from the book, Jurisdiction Three. We have spoken of Harmony, and we have said much regarding Abundance, and I step forth to give you the third discourse on Clarity.

Dear hearts, first Harmony then Abundance, what would be the next step of this natural course? Clarity. For you see, the millenium that we enter into, what we have planned for over five thousand years, is a period of time to be sustained. Do you understand what a momentous occasion this would be? To sustain eternal, universal law? This has not occurred on your planet. Do you understand, Dear ones?

Question: "It has never occurred?"

Dear one, it has never been sustained. It has occurred, yes. But it has never been sustained.

May I proceed?

Response: "Yes."

WHAT IS THE LIGHT?

Clarity.

What is the light? It is simple to say that the light is Clarity, but let us examine what the light truly is. The light shines through man and man at times holds this light. The light shines through your Brother and your Sister. And your Brother and Sister sometimes hold this light. You gaze upon the light. You look at the light. You speak of the light. You hear the light. But do you know what the light is?

The light has come forth for Clarity, Dear one. It has come forth not to judge. It has come forth not to discern. It has come forth simply to be. It is Clarity. The light helps you to clearly see. It helps you to clearly hear. It helps you to clearly be. You are creative beings Dear ones. And you are allowed to see clearly.

Much that has occurred upon your planet is the result of lack of the use of the tool, light, and lack of Clarity. When individuals see clearly, is not their intent an alignment with their will? When individuals can see clearly, have they not brought into balance Divine Love? When individuals see clearly, they recognize the purpose of their life and question no more. For you see, then, Dear ones, there are answers to all questions, for the choices are clearly seen and heard. Do you understand Dear one?

Response: "Yes."

APPLY EACH JURISDICTIONS IN SEQUENCE, ONE AT A TIME

So the Third Jurisdiction, which is called Clarity, is presented to bring light to the interactions of human beings, the interaction of humanity to the Beloved I AM Presence, and the Beloved I AM Presence to that of the Creator of Creators. To step forth as a creative being, one must understand what it is like to sustain the distribution of energies for creative flow. You speak of Harmony and Balance, but have no agreement. You speak of Abundance, and have no Harmony. You speak of Clarity, and have no prosperity. Dear ones, they build upon the other, one to the next. Jacob's ladder, what was it? It was for you to understand that the universe was built step by step.

And so we enter into this period of time, a period of time brought to the point of sustaining. Do you have your questions Dear one?

Question: "Are you complete with this discourse?"

It is a simple discourse. They are simple words.

Question: "And the names of these discourses, what should we call them all?"

Millenium Fundamentals, Dear one.

Question: "I understand. Now, you are asking and teaching at the same time, are you not?"

This is true, Dear one.

Question: "You are asking that we master these Jurisdictions?"

It is important, Dear ones, that you step forward as a creative being of this period of time. For we have spoken much of the example.

Question: "I understand. You are asking us to master and to set an example as your messengers?"

For you see, Dear one, third density beings only understand what they can touch.

Question: "I understand that, but for the record, in fourth density, all beings resonating at like frequency are able to touch, are they not?"

When I refer to third density, I refer to only that density. Yes it is true. We are able to touch, to see, to smell and at greater intensity. However, we have refined.

Question: "I understand. But do you not still have a body?"

At will, we do.

Question: "But it does not serve your purpose at the more refined densities, does it?"

It is impossible to carry it into the higher energetic sources.

Question: "Then it just expands, doesn't it . . . from my third density perception?"

From your third density perception, expansion is a creative wave, taken from the eighth layer to the fifteenth.

Question: "And you are about ready to complete the fifteenth?"

That is the consolidation point which is achieved by the balance of duplication and expansion.

Response: "I am most pleased to be of Service to you always."

And it is I who am pleased to serve you, Dear ones.

Response: "I thank you whole heartedly for your patience with us. Sometimes it is difficult to understand."

Dear one, remember I am available for questioning. I serve you, and it is my desire to bring this to clarification. Do you see I am not exempt. I, too, practice. Do you understand?

Response: "Yes. For I am your representative in this density. And I also must be of Service to everyone around me."

You are most blessed and thanked for what you do. Clarity is a topic in your time over which there has been much storm and fuss. It is very simple, Dear one.

Question: "Clarity is the inner light that each of us carries?"

When one has understood and built to this point of choice, he sees without hesitation. There is no question. There is choice, yes! When you are thirsty, what do you drink?

Response: "Clear water."

When you are hungry, what do you eat?

Response: "The fruits of the garden, for they are also clear."

EVERYONE IS OF THE LIGHT

We address your planet, which has come forth Brother against Brother, Sister against Sister, family fighting within the family. Is this one clear? Does this one hold light? Dear ones, do you see, you all use the light and are of the light!

Question: "It has been my observation that everyone is of the light, but has forgotten. I look at them and all I can see is to allow them to be who they are, to just accept them."

Remember, as I said to you, be the open window.

Response: "That has been most helpful."

And now I say, be not the open window, be the open door. Allow more light to flow through you, Dear one. We shall enter into the principle for discourse which I'm sure you know will follow, the Law Of Love.

Response: "The law which binds all the universes together."

Dear one, do you have more questions?

Response: "On Clarity? No, I find a peacefulness with that. I thank you for this discourse."

I shall take my rest and invite you too, to do so. Dear Brother you are always welcome at my side. I AM Sananda. I AM AT YOUR SERVICE!

CHAPTER TWENTY-EIGHT
Sananda presents the Fourth Jurisdiction

Love

The Law of Allowing, Maintenance, and Sustainability

"Love is the first action and energy to come forth in creation."
- SANANDA

We begin in prayer:

Great Light of Divine Wisdom, stream forth to my being and through your right use let me serve mankind and the planet. Love from the heart of God, radiate my being with the presence of the Christ, that I walk the path of truth. Great source of creation, empower my being, my Brother, my Sister, and my planet as we collectively awaken as ONE Cell. I call forth the Cellular Awakening. Let wisdom, love, and power stream forth to this Cell, this Cell that we all share. So we may share the ONE perfected Cell, I AM.

And continue with the invocation:

Beloved host of Ascended Masters, Beloved Sananda, Saint Germain, Kuthumi, El Morya, and any of those who wish to facilitate this morning, please come forth. Please bring your discourse to us. We thank you so much. We are in your Service now and always.

Beloved Mighty I AM Presence, come forth. Great Host of Ascended Masters, Beloved Sananda, Beloved Saint Germain, Beloved Mirananda, Beloved Kuthumi and El Morya. Soltec, Mary, and Kuan Yin, come forth Dear ones. I give you permission to enter into my energy field, so we may continue your work upon this planet.

Response: "I also give you permission to enter into my energy field, so you may come forth and bring us this information."

Greetings Dear one, and in the heart of the most radiant ONE, I too come! I AM Sananda, and am most blessed to be one to do this work with you. For you see, Dear one, before we read the next lesson from this book of the Province, it is important that you understand that discipline within itself is, again, a principle of Love. It is what contains within itself an orderliness, that is a pattern and repeats itself over and over again. Within its consciousness is the consciousness of Love, that Love which comes forth from the heart of God as you speak, and continues to flow eternally.

It is now important that you record this room. To my right is my Beloved Brother Saint Germain. He has stepped forth in this age to sponsor this transitional work upon your Earth Plane and Planet. He came forth previously to set this flame upon the Earth Plane and Planet. He is, indeed, the Chohan of the Seventh Ray, which brings forth transformation of the individual, and combines the work of the Pink Ray and the Blue Ray, into the Beloved Violet Ray of Transformation and the LAW OF GRACE!

To my other side stands Beloved Archangel Michael, protector of this universe, he who stepped forth to also sponsor this age, to protect this planet, so that TRUTH would reign supreme within the hearts of man. He, too, is there to call upon during this time. For he too, like you, Dear ones, has stepped forth to sponsor, and all serve in their capacity. Each gives what they may give. And he too has offered to give up his position, should this mission fail. For you see, it is the collective energy that comes forth that we are able to work upon. It is what is held as a reserve that we draw upon. Energy must come forth, sponsored from each Ray.

Dear one, we sit now at our desk, this desk that we call the Throne at the Foot of God. For, indeed, this is information which comes from the feet of THE HOLY OF HOLIES, the Alpha and the Omega, the Creator of Creators. It is brought to be held by the Creator of your universe, whom you know as Apollo. This book comes, indeed, beyond that.

ALLOWING SUSTAINS AND MAINTAINS LOVE

Jurisdiction Four: The Book of Love

Love is indeed from the heart of God and it travels as a stream. It is the light that allows all to flow within the universe. God commanded Love from his lips and from this came light. And so you see, Dear ones, the command came first, and the principle of all creation is Love. Throughout your histories, one has pondered this which is called Love. It has been interpreted in many ways. Love is indeed the first creative action; it is what is, and creatively sustains life, in a creative way. This is indeed Love. And we shall look at what sustains and nurtures Love.

Allowance is important. Allowing has been associated with this great creative way of being. Allowing complements the energy known as Love, for Love can then stream forth. LOVE FROM THE HEART OF GOD STREAM FORTH! It is a direct line, a direct Ray. Its purpose and directive is to create and then sustain, which brings us to the next principle regarding Love, sustaining Love.

FEMININE LOVE MAINTAINS, THE MALE SUSTAINS

Through allowance, the clear path is established, but Love must then be maintained and sustained. Maintenance is natural for many upon your planet. It comes forth from the feminine principle. It is nurturing and allows growth. Maintenance is the maternal energy that steps forth and says, "I have allowed this Love to come forth, this creative energy; I will maintain it, carrying it in my being." This is a step of creation.

MASCULINE LOVE SUSTAINS AND PROTECTS

Then the masculine principle steps forth to sustain. It protects and says, "I will create a space and home so this shall be sustained."

You see, Dear ones, you have Love, which guards the first principle of creation. This creative principle contains within it the feminine and masculine principles and travels forth on allowance. It comes forth no other way!

LOVE AND CREATION

For you see, Dear one, Love may not enter your planet without choice. The hearts of men must allow Love to stream forth. They must choose for this Love to be allowed to stream forth, to and from their hearts. The origin of this great energy called Love comes from the Supreme Creator. And as perpetual motion, it maintains and sustains itself when applied and used with these principles.

Love is the first energy allowed to come forth in creation. Its application and understanding have long been misinterpreted on your planet. However, it is our hope that one day it shall stream forth to all upon your planet! For it is indeed the tie that binds each, not only to his Beloved Creator, to his Beloved Mighty I AM Presence, and to his Beloved Family, but it is the tie that binds him to what he too has created. Then man steps forth truly as a Creator in the image and likeness of that I AM THAT I AM, A BEING OF LOVE.

Response: "This is most beautiful. And I thank you very much for bringing this forth."

Dear one, it is in Love that we come. Do you not see we stream forth from the heart of the Holy of Holies? We stream forth on that fiery breath. Love comes forth from the Eternal Logos.

Response: "Yes, it is the binding force which makes space for all creation to happen."

Dear one, do you have more questions?

Question: "Yes, I think we need to clarify that Love really is not an emotion, that it is an energy."

It is indeed such. If you would only look at the activity that you do, and call it Love. The activity of Love streams forth, eternally sustained, eternally maintained, and ever achieving!

Response: "When Love is viewed as an emotion, it can be overwhelming energetically, instead of making space for creativity?"

This is true, Dear one, and being clouded with emotion disqualifies creative energy. Love comes forth to bring greater clarity. Do you not see how the Law of Love was built on the Law of Clarity? For Love must stream forth. It must be able to stream forth into clear space.

Response: "Yes."

The Jurisdictions have come to serve as great Principles of Being. They have been structured in a manner and way that is the easiest to use. These are, indeed, practiced methods. We do not sit here and endlessly give out these principles; they are tried and true, and practiced by all of us within this universe, of course, with the exception of this planet.

The time is at hand, Dear one! The time has come! Mankind must understand that there is much more at stake then merely this planet. Yes, Dear one, we have much compassion; however, there is a pattern that has come forth in this universe as a creative wave. The angels now glorify this pattern and sing the choir, Let Love Stream Forth to the Hearts of Men Forever!

May I be of further assistance?

BEYOND LOVE'S PASSION: TOLERANCE AND AGREEMENT

Question: "What many call Love may actually be an attraction of like or similar resonance. But this resonance can use the energy of Love to create?"

They are acting specifically on allowance and it is that Ray which streams forth. These two beings have interacted in a creative way through what is called "allow." Allow contains within it principles that you know as tolerance and agreement. For you see, Dear one, maintenance and sustenance cannot come forth without clear use of previous cosmic laws, as I am sure you are well aware. And, yes, mankind does indeed see Love as passion. But passion is only the urge to allow Love to stream forth from the Heart Of God.

Love is the beginning and it is the end. However, see it as the beginning step of creation. Let Love be the beginning word to grace the lips, as did Beloved Apollo when he came forth to sponsor your Sun.

THE PURPOSE OF THE JURISDICTIONS

Dear one, step forth as the Blessed Being that you are. Realize your purpose in being here is to allow this Mighty Energy to come forth! Not only for others, but for your creative wave and work upon this planet. Which leads us Dear one to the next chapter.

Response: "Please proceed."

Dear one, it is Service. However, it is important that you carefully review the first four Jurisdictions. We are still available to answer your questions.

Response: "I am still concerned about emotions that are out of control when Love is misunderstood and how this clouds clarity."

Dear one, they are only the end result of not applying the first three Jurisdictions. It is important with each of these Jurisdictions that they are applied to build upon each other. For what are these Jurisdictions if they are not understood and applied? In your world of thought and feeling, the e-motion can cloud the Creatorship. Do you understand?

Response: "Yes. Then it would make sense that we set these first four to paper, for review and study."

It is important that you understand what we say to you, for we too are building, step by step, a vibration to come through.

These Jurisdictions have never been released in their entirety to your planet. As they come forth, they indeed set a foundation which you may refer to as the World Constitution, which we refer to as Jurisdictions. They are laws which we honor; their application is tried and true.

Response: "I ask only that when we do what we call editing, which is clarification of sentence structure, that we are guided."

Call upon me, Dear one, and I shall be there. Call upon Beloved Saint Germain, for he shall be there. Call upon Beloved Archangel Michael, for he shall be there. When two or more are gathered in my name, I AM THAT I AM, I AM THERE!

OUR PRECIOUS TIME ON EARTH

Dear one, I understand your great need and thirst for knowledge of the universe, for I too contained within my heart, a great burst of creative desire when I was in your shoes.

Question: "Do you really remember being here?"

Dear one, how could I forget what served me well. My time spent upon your Earth Plane and Planet is a treasure to me. I also remember well being within the density. Do you not remember being a tree? Do you not remember the stillness of the air? The stillness of water? Dear one, I too remember the stillness of your world, and respect and cherish what was given to me in great Love.

Dear one, may we conclude?

Response: "Yes we may. I love you."

I LOVE YOU DEAR ONE, STEP FORTH AS THE GLORIOUS GOD-FREE BEINGS THAT YOU ARE! STEP FORTH IN THE MAGNIFICENCE OF THE COMING AGE! I AM THAT I AM.

Response: "I thank you for all that you have given and done this morning."

CHAPTER TWENTY-NINE
Sananda presents the Fifth Jurisdiction

Service

The Law of Love

"Love, in Service, breathes the breath for all."
- SANAT KUMARA

The Fifth Jurisdiction for our Province, once known as Prahna, now known as Terra.

I'm walking up a long set of stairs. They are all white, and I'm coming to a platform suspended within a dimension. There is a host of Archangels. Archangel Michael is to my left, Saint Germain to my right. Seated is Sanat Kumara, and Sananda is standing behind him. He has opened to these golden pages again. He is motioning me to come forward and he asks,

Shall I proceed?

Response: "Please, Dear ones, proceed. I thank you for coming to bring this Jurisdiction to us this morning."

SERVICE RELEASES POWER

Greetings Dear one. I AM Sanat Kumara, otherwise known as your ancestral Grandfather, who has brought you forth in sponsorship to continue this work. For it is in the continuation of this work, that you have chosen to bring forth, that you have allowed yourself to be of Service. And it is through this Jurisdiction that this Service comes forth, as an understanding that you are the Service itself.

Service is the sharing. It is the exchange. It is the alignment. It is the allowing, the giving. It is the precious life that each carries. It is the light. It is the sound. It is everything that we are. It is the pivot point of all creation. It is the focal point from which we do this work; it is the greatest of all desire.

Service is very much confused with taking a power, instead of releasing a power. Service is very much confused, as when one serves, one supposes one will be, as you say, remunerated. But Service is the alignment. It is the allowing. It is the sharing. It is the giving of all without expectation; the law of the universe will provide!

Do you have a question?

GIVE WITHOUT EXPECTATION

Question: "And so Service is what we give without expectation?"

FIFTH JURISDICTION: SERVICE

This is true. It is the exchange of energy without the expectation that you are to be built above the station that you are at in the moment of exchange.

Question: "So in Service we give without expectation of energetic balance?"

There is truly energetic balance in the giving of the Service. Were you not given initially, the breath of life? And is this not a creative flow? As you give, do you not exchange, and does it not come back? It is the expectation that will create for you a dis-Service.

Question: "And so Service is formed at a level of agreement that is more universal?"

Service is agreement, for it is born in agreement. The same agreement that comes from the heart's desire that aligns with Love. The same agreement that allows one to continue on. It allows the even flow, the exchange, the understanding. The Love that creates! Service is born of Love!

Response: "You explain this to be a gentle act."

Most assuredly it is a gentle act. It is an avenue, if you will, of the expression of the creativity of Love.

Question: "So Service is another expression of Love?"

SERVICE IS AN EXPRESSION OF LOVE

It is indeed. It is an expression of the creative wave of the cycle of the circle, the expansion. It continues on, infinitely, it continues on and creates. It is what fuels the flame for continuous breath. It goes on and on for as long as one can expand. Service is what we all choose in the expansion of ourselves. It is the step, one at a time that we take, that we agree to take, and that we bring forth, based on the Love that we are.

Response: "I understand."

So, in giving this Service you become part of the creative cycle. You are as you truly are. For it is from Service that all life springs. It is the well, it is the eternal flowing, if you will, of Love. For Love, if it is contained, is not love. And it breathes no breath of eternity. But Love, in Service, breathes the breath for all. It breathes the life and the light. It is the sound.

Response: "I see what you are saying. It is an expansive exhale."

Most truly it is. This Service that we choose is the path of all of us. We, when we come to you, come to you to be of Service. It is the expression of who we are. It is the expression of who this planet is: Service. It is the actual functioning of the love that comes forth from the fiery breath of I AM THAT I AM. Without this Service there is no expression or expansion. There is no creativity. All cycles stop. So as you have offered yourself in Service, so do we reciprocate? For that is as the law is stated.

Service, the continuous growth, brings forth light and Love. And it flows on the sound of the E. It is as you have noted in your A, E, I, O, and U sounds, it flows on the E of motion, as opposed to the O of motion. These are just energetic patterns, which through sound has an avenue. service wells up in your human heart to be of help, to be of assistance. Service on this planet, once again, is the expansive energy on the E phrase of the motions of life or the motions of creation.

Question: "And so it works on qualified emotion, is what you are saying?"

Qualified emotional activity, in your density.

Response: "I see. Thank you. Proceed."

SHARE FROM YOUR HEART

Service is the point when one has allowed alignment to give all and expect nothing. To be aligned, is to find your heart, and to find the Love that creates your heart. Then share that heart in Service. It is a creative expansion.

Question: "I understand. Do you have more?"

This completes what Service is for this province. We are here, all of us, as have been summoned in Service, to answer your questions.

Question: "Thank you Beloved Sanat Kumara. It is wonderful to be in your presence. Service is a creative expansion of the desire of the heart. It is a natural flow. When individuals are aligned with their heart's desire they express this outwardly in a way that it rubs off on another? Is this correct?"

Rubs off? That is one way to put it! The energetic pattern is seated throughout all of the bodies of your energy patterns. You see, as you become more of Service, you become more of creation. The Cosmic Beings that you refer to, whom you do not see in embodiment, are those who have held the continuum of Service. They have stayed at certain energetic patterns of expressions of Service, by choice, by choice based on the Law of Love. So each Service that you do master, brings you further and further to fulfill each of the energetic bodies that you have. You come forward in Service. You give your life in Service. You share and create in Service. Then the Service comes back to you.

Question: "So you are saying that Service is an energetic pattern of creation within each and every one of us. Is this so?"

It is the energetic pattern of expansion.

Question: "Is this creative pattern indivdualized?"

FIFTH JURISDICTION: SERVICE

SERVICE IS MULTIFACETED AND HAS MULTIPLE EXPRESSIONS

Each DNA structure that is augmented or, if you will, diminished, or co-changing from one genetic structure to another, is ingrained with a Service coding. And this Service coding follows certain patterns that are established in the Divine Realm. These Service patterns allow each DNA structure to function on each of the Rays that you have discovered. The Service patterns are a coding frequency which allows each of the Rays to resonate through each of the patterns. For when your Service coding of the Green Ray comes in contact with that of the Pink Ray, the coding does resonate, but does not necessarily align into that Service. But it does resonate in a harmonic. Do you see?

Response: "So, when persons are aligned with heart's desire to serve, this resonates with their DNA coding?"

This is precise. Have you noticed that each one chooses a different resonance of Service? For many parts of creation do create the whole. It is the agreement of the Service that brings forth the Abundance that brings forth the prosperity and most assuredly the illumination.

Response: "I do have a question regarding the cellular coding, or the Cellular Awakening."

Proceed.

Question: "Through Service are we able to change DNA coding to cellular coding?"

It is one avenue. It is one path. The cellular coding is a function of the DNA structure. It contains the Service enzyme. The Service electromagnetic patterns allow for expansion. For it is only in Service that expansion occurs. Expansion, then, creates new patterns which allow the ones which do not resonate harmonically to be consumed by the Violet Flame. These inharmonic patterns, when consumed and transmuted by the Violet Flame, then become aligned.

Response: "Oh, I see. You are saying that the one type of activity that will expand energy, is the energetic exchange of Service."

Yes.

Question: "And, as you have explained, Service is what you give without expecting?"

Look at the historical accounts of all Masters who have been in your density. Have they not given Service without expectation?

Response: "It would appear to be that way."

But by doing that, have they not broken the pattern that exists in all negotiations in your density, where one expects something from another for an exchange? You see, the exchange is the balance. But the expectation creates a pattern that inhibits Service without expectation. For those who are in the need, or requirement of exchange, resonate in a frequency that does not expand beyond the exchange.

It is a pattern. This is not to say that certain things do not automatically exchange. Service without expectation is automatically exchanged. It brings forth your inner light. It brings forth your illumination. It builds your energetic bodies. It moves you into the realm of expansion. There is no loss. There is nothing wasted.

Response: "Thank you, Dear one. This has been a beautiful discourse and has touched me very deeply."

CHAPTER THIRTY
Sananda presents the Sixth Jurisdiction

Illumination

Live without Fear or Judgment

*"Illumination, yes, is an action of your mind!
Illumination is the use of your mind
without fear and judgment."*
- SANAT KUMARA

Welcome my Beloved chelas, I AM Sananda. I cord myself to you, heart to heart. For you see, Dear ones, these Jurisdictions speak not to the minds of men, but speak to the heart of the illuminated being that you are to become. I come to you again from the Council Table. Archangel Michael and Beloved Saint Germain stand on either side of me as I give forth this information. Beloved Sanat Kumara has left to prepare Jurisdictions eight and nine. And I give forth number six, Illumination.

"BE" WITH KNOWING AND NON-JUDGMENT

The bond with God is arranged in harmony with the thoughts of men. It is a symphony that is conducted and arranged from the proper use of energy upon your planet. Throughout the eons there have been many expressions of thought, thought being an intangible wave and energetic pattern upon your planet. There are, indeed, thoughts that come from the creative Source, and there are those that come from the source known as the ego. When you begin to understand the world of the mind, you see the mind operates with only one law, and that is choice. The choice to choose creatively or the choice to choose non-creatively. This is the choice between the creative state and the ego state. You have known this to be simply that of non-judgment versus judgment.

When you come to the point that your energetic thinking patterns have been used in a way of non-judgment, you enter into the action of Illumination. Illumination has long been misunderstood upon your planet. One thinks, if I think more this way or that way I shall have more choice. I shall have more information. And when one comes to me, I shall give this out. Dear ones, you must understand, Illumination comes not from knowing, but from being your knowing. It is the choice which was made from the first law of this universe. The choice of allowing Love to stream forth. Illumination comes forth into the minds of men set through the energetic pattern of being without judgment.

A MIND WITHOUT FEAR

There has been much talk upon your planet of enlightenment. Many scramble, searching for more enlightenment. You see, Dear ones, enlightenment you all have! You all carry the flame within your hearts; however, you must uncover it, and allow the clean air to fan its embers so it may glow. Enlightenment is not an action of the mind; enlightenment is the light which is carried as one becomes aligned in the seventh energetic body.

Illumination, yes, it is indeed an action of your mind! Illumination is the choice you make to use your mind without fear and without judgment. It allows the free flow of the life force, again, the continuous breath, to come into your thinking. And this affects your being and your doing. See, Dear ones, Illumination, again, is an action! The action of Service expands, and Illumination is the action of rhythmically duplicating the expanding process of being. Each of these Jurisdictions have been brought forth for you to choose from.

Each of them comes with an energetic action. Illumination, you may choose, and it is a very simple act. It allows for your light to come forth through choice, and sets the stage for creation. Do you have questions?

Question: "Illumination is an act of choice, knowing the Law of Love. Is this correct?"

It is based upon the Law of Love, for when one asks with an aligned heart, one is illumined to one's great part in the universe.

Response: "I see. And in that respect, each and every one of us, incarnate and not incarnate, is a great part in the universe."

THE ILLUMINED MIND WORKS FOR THE ONE

It is a symphony, Dear one. Each thought that streams forth from the mind of man is a note. Each note comes forth to form an idea. And how does action come forth? It is the interplay of ideas! Of idea and idea. The ideas form a chord bonded on the strings of Harmony and agreement. An illumined mind understands that each thought that comes forth plays a part and maintains the Law of Agreement and the Law of Harmony. An illumined mind understands that, through choice, one may become a part of the symphony. All have their part to play. Have you heard a symphony composed only of solos?

Response: "Never, Dear one."

Each plays a part. Each carries a note and collective action. Illumination calls for responsible action in choice.

Response: "This I do see, for the choice is based on a knowingness and acceptance of responsibility of the choice."

While it would appear that choosing is done alone and playing a solo part, the illumined mind chooses knowing the note to be played is part of this grand composition. To understand timing and orderliness is to understand Harmony and positioning. To understand that arrangement is not built upon being the loudest, the most magnificent, the most knowing, the most grandiose. The illumined mind understands the creative interplay for a work of beauty to come forth. It holds at all time the work of creative beauty

SIXTH JURISDICTION: ILLUMINATION

first, and asks "Does this thought serve this end?" Dear one, mankind has long seen enlightenment as the way to build the self. The illumined mind works to build not only itself but creation. May I serve you further?

Response: "I do understand this, Dear one. If you so choose, you may retire, or continue."

Illumination sets the stage of choice. For the next Jurisdiction, number seven, is indeed one of the most important upon your planet, Cooperation. For the sake of this Jurisdiction, it shall come forth in two parts. Cooperation contains masculine and feminine interpretations. Do you understand?

Response: "I understand."

Dear one, I take my rest from your frequency. I hold you in my heart. I AM Sananda.

Response: "And I hold you in mine, my Beloved."

CHAPTER THIRTY-ONE
Lady Master Venus presents the
Seventh Jurisdiction: the Feminine Principle of

Cooperation

Live with Beauty and Honor

*"Beauty sees the exquisite boundaries of each individual.
Cooperation sees the form of divinity first,
and then honors the function."*
- LADY MASTER VENUS

Greetings Beloved children of the Golden Sun. I AM known as Lady Master Venus, and I require your permission to enter your energy fields.

Response: "Please do come forth into this energy field and come and share with us."

I come to you from the planet we know as the Garden, and I come to give you discourse. I have been asked to present the feminine principle of Cooperation.

She is sitting on a bench in a garden. To her left side is Archangel Michael and to her right is Sananda. Behind her is Saint Germain, and Archangel Michael is handing her the book, "Jurisdictions for the Province."

SEE BEAUTY IN ALL THINGS

Dear ones, I may read and present this material to you; however, it is the perspective I come to bring to you, for I have embodied the perfection of feminine Cooperation. I come from the planetary system that you share, and I come from the planet known as Venus. For on our planet, we have understood the principles of Cooperation. This was how we have been able to express and sustain Harmony, balance, and beauty for well over three million years, as you would measure time. It was not through luck that this occurred or through chance; there were, indeed, many times that we failed, and we worked again. I'll open these pages and read, but first you must understand, Cooperation is a work that comes forth. It is not a magic formula, it is two who work their energies together.

COOPERATION

There was a time upon your planet when all cooperated with one another. The animals cooperated with the plants. The Plant or vegetable Kingdom cooperated with the Mineral Kingdom. The Mineral Kingdom cooperated with the Devas and Elementals. All knew, in the scope of their kingdoms, that they held divinity within their Spirit, and worried not if they had less or more.

A day fell upon your planet when each kingdom from vegetable, mineral, animal, and even humankind doubted their divinity. Mistrust swept through each kingdom. Great quarrels and bickerings erupted and the peaceful way of life eroded and was no longer.

SEVENTH JURISDICTION: FEMININE COOPERATION

What is this that has happened, Dear children? A collective forgetting, as you have called it? A doubt which came within their hearts that they were not divine. This doubt spread, that they were not really who they were. And the Plant Kingdom said to the Mineral Kingdom, "I will take what is mine, for you do not exist!" And the human said, "I will take what is mine, for you are not real!" Cooperation honors the beauty of all things. Cooperation, as a feminine principle, also honors the beauty of all things and it sees within life the majestic qualities that maintain beauty.

You may ask, "Is beauty only what is judged from one to the next?" Beauty sees the exquisite boundaries of each individual. To cooperate is to honor form and then honor function. To cooperate is to hold this above all, to see divinity first, and function second. We again ask for you to see the Divine Spark in all. It was told to you that you live and breathe and walk in a world of Spirit. Dear children, you live and breathe and walk in a world of divinity. All that is around you is divine!

To cooperate holds this law, the Law of Divine Beauty, first. When two enter into an agreement to cooperate they hold the picture of Divine Beauty. They see the spark that each one carries. One should never interfere with another's divinity. You live in a world of turmoil, and we come from a world of beauty. The difference? Above all, we honor divinity. Any agreement that is entered into is seen through the eyes of the maintenance of divinity. Dear ones, this concept is not foreign to you! You know it is a simple truth. It is the maintenance of such a truth that seems to take the Wisdom of Ages. Is not your planet ready for the Wisdom of Ages to come forth? Have you not waited long enough, Dear children? I ask for you to surround yourself in the world of what you truly are.

I ask for you to step into the Flame of your Divinity and be what you are! And others around you shall become such. You are divine, Dear ones; there is no doubt to that. The doubt you carry of your divinity is to be removed. Do you have questions?

ABOUT DOUBT AND JUDGMENT

Question: "Yes, where did the doubt come from?"

You saw who you were. Doubt comes from judgment.

Question: "Does judgment have a source? Who taught us to be judgmental?"

You are made in the image and likeness of the Creator. It has long been said that you have been given free will; however, we prefer to look at it differently. It is not a matter of your free will, it is the matter of an exploring, inquisitive mind. And mind you, a mind is not your heart! For the heart never forgets. It was the Mental Body which doubted the existence of perfection, and has willingly perceived that a creation could be less then perfect.

May I assist you, Dear one?

Response: "Yes, you are reading my energy. Thank you for offering. The confusing part is that we are operating from this perspective in the Mental Body."

Cease your judgment, Dear one. For all creation is perfected. All creation holds within it the Divine Spark. Cease your judgment, Dear one, for an instant, and look beyond this veil (maya). Do you not see the garden you live in?

Response: "Yes."

Are not all the Rays present in their glory? Does not each kingdom function on its pitch and hue?

Response: "Yes."

Is this not orchestrated before you in perfection? For the Creator of Creators has given you His world. You are a Divine Being, Dear one. You have come to cooperate with All That Is.

It has been said that when a house is built, the foundation determines how strong the structure is. Is this not so?

Response: "Yes."

But you know well that each individual board also contributes. Each nail contributes. Each gives of its divinity. Each cooperates from the Flame of Divine Perfection, and the end result is beauty.

Response: "Yes, balance, Harmony, all of these."

Dear one, to cooperate is to hold and maintain the structure of beauty, to honor the Divine Spark in All That Is.

Response: "To carry the vision of the divinity always."

To never lose that focus. The work of Cooperation is to carry a strong focus at all times! The feminine principle is to recognize the beauty of divinity in all things. I AM Lovingly Yours.

Response: "I AM Lovingly Yours also."

CHAPTER THIRTY-TWO
Sanat Kumara presents the
Seventh Jurisdiction: the Masuline Principle of

Cooperation

Live with Beauty and Honor

"It is the sustaining in this cooperation that allows the harmonics of Creation to flow forward, so that you and all are ONE."
- SANAT KUMARA

Greetings my Beloved divine children! I AM Sanat Kumara. Do I have your permission to come forth?

Response: "Yes, Dear one."

COOPERATION IS BOTH PART AND WHOLE

I am here to continue discourse on Cooperation. This is the balance of the masculine and feminine energetic patterns. This agreement exists in all of creation, for the sustaining of creation is upon agreement. Agreement, Cooperation, and balance are, at times, interchangeable and, at others, separate and definable, but always functioning within the resonance of expansion. In Cooperation you do bring forth the agreement. In Cooperation you do follow through and sustain. It is the sustaining in this Cooperation that allows the harmonics of creation to flow forward, so that you and all are ONE.

Do you see how a cooperative thought expands because the cooperative thought is a focus? It requires the energetic patterning of more than one pattern. It is the focus of this pattern that duplicates. In its expansion it duplicates from one to another and creates an expansion that is a duplication and a duplication that is an expansion. As one fills, the other empties; and another fills and another empties. It continues on and on. It is a basic law of how creation has come about and how it functions. The sustaining of Cooperation is the lesson and the focal point of your upcoming 1,000 year period.

Cooperation is called forth through all the energetic layers of your planet, from the interior to the exterior. It is being called forth for all who inhabit every region of consciousness. The focus of Cooperation is always sustained because we have the desire to sustain Cooperation. The first step in this sustaining, as the great Lady Master Venus has given to you, is non-judgment. For what is, is! And you are part of this, and you are the whole of it at the same time. For as you expand, you become whole! Become whole and realize your part.

IMMORTAL, TIMELESS DIVINITY

Here, in this sustaining, is the masculine quality that is being brought forth now. Sustaining is an energetic pattern that you can choose and you can share and you can allow. I am here as an example of the sustaining. For in the time on Venus, it took much to bring about sustaining. It took much to bring this Cooperation to a point where the struggle was released and the allowing came forward in non-judgment; then the energy of divinity would circulate and be in the consciousness of all who are here. This consciousness that you ask for is the illumination of the divinity. It is the knowing, the seeing, the being that you truly are! Here and now and always are the same! There is no difference. Your divinity is here and now and always, and is the same.

THE UNCHANGEABLE

Your forgetting is just the path that you have chosen. But now it is your time. It is your cycle to choose remembering your divinity and sustaining the understanding that this divinity is not denied in the most minutest of the atomic structures to the most grandiose of the seas. Your planet is divine. All are part of the whole, and in being whole they do their part. You, my Dear ones, children of the Golden Flame, the Golden Flame of Creation is the pivot point of this Eighth Ray from which all is balanced. You, my children, are divine! You are Love! You are the image and likeness of the great I AM THAT I AM! You are the image and likeness of the power of all powers. You are complete, and you are part, and you are whole.

Sustain this vision of self! Sustain this vision of your own individuation. Sustain this vision of all. Sustain this vision of the minute speck of dust! Divinity is there. Sustain this vision of everything, everyone and everywhere, every time, and you will then be doing your part of the whole. Come forward and announce your own divinity to yourself in the quietness of your heart, and announce your own divinity to all around you. Sustain and hold the focus, and you will then carry the light that you truly are.

Your enlightenment has always been and will always be. That is unchangeable. Bring your conscious awareness, your focus, to the sustaining, and cooperate with yourself in this great magnificence that you are. Cooperate with all others in the great magnificence that they are. You are here because of your great desire. You are expressing because of your great nature. You are here because of Love. You are expressing because you are that you are: complete, pure, divine, eternal, All Love is you. Do you have a question?

Question: "Thank you Sanat Kumara, I have no questions. But if you would clarify this point for me, I would appreciate it. In essence, you are saying that, in order to cooperate, that this veil, this separation needs to be removed in order for us to see one another's light, is this so?"

You call this veil a separation. We call this a pattern of judgment. Carry the vision of your divinity and the creation you all have shared in, then your veil of separation will be dissolved. Carry the vision you are divine. Carry the vision that everyone else is as you are.

SEVENTH JURISDICTION: MASCULINE COOPERATION

Question: "Then, the Masculine Principle of Cooperation is to sustain?"

It is to carry, which creates sustaining. It is to carry the inner light and to share the illumined inner light, which is the representation of the divinity. For the light which is inner, is the light that is without, and it is all encompassing and all expanding.

The sound carries forth on the frequency of the thought that you have, for each thought has an intonation. When one thinks less than divinity, sound is carried forth through the inner light and is brought forth to the outer. The outer is where the consciousness chooses to focus and that focus is then reflected to the inner. This creates what you have had, struggle and judgment. When the thought from the Mental Body carries the frequency, the intonation, of divinity and takes that thought and runs through that same process, then the doubt that had once been the conscious focus is diminished.

It is a choice to focus on the thought that all are divine. As one chooses this focus, the divinity is expressed. Then Cooperation is manifest, for in divinity there is perfection.

Question: "So the lesson is to keep our focus on divinity and this will result in Cooperation?"

The continuing result of carrying this focus of thought of all being divine is Cooperation.

Question: "And so Cooperation is an energetic pattern to be carried. It is not an end result?"

This is true.

Response: "Thank you Dear one."

If you have no other questions, we shall retire, and at the appropriate call come forward.

Response: "I thank you and Lady Master Venus for coming forth this morning for discourse."

CHAPTER THIRTY-THREE
Sanat Kumara presents the Eighth Jurisdiction

Charity

Live with Love and Equity

"Charity is a distribution, and it is the equalizer when there is injustice and inequity."
- SANAT KUMARA

I call forth the great Hosts of Ascended Masters: the Great White Brotherhood, the Divine Brotherhood, the Celestial Brotherhood, the Cosmic Brotherhood. I call forth all of those of the Angelic Realm. And I ask for access and permission to be of Service.

Once again, I am ascending the steps into the marble room that is back-lighted. I see Saint Germain to my right, Archangel Michael to my left. Sanat Kumara is again seated at the desk. Sananda is behind him, standing to his right. I come forward as he motions, and he asks me to kneel. As I kneel a chair appears. I am seated across from him.

Greetings. Beloved chelas, children of the Golden Flame. I AM Sanat Kumara, keeper of this work and bearer of this expansion. May I come forth in the completeness?

After giving my permission, I made the request that Len be allowed to scan him energetically and give a description, so that others may understand how he appears.

You have seen him in more than one appearance, which one do you choose?

Response: "Whichever one you prefer, Dear one, for your readers to see. I give that choice to you."

He is changing from his rather distinguished self to an eternal energy of youth. His skin is white gold. The robe that he wears covers his left shoulder but the right one is bare. His robe comes right below the knees. He wears gold laced sandals and gold trim around the bottom of his robe. There is gold trim also at the arms and the neck. There is a gold clasp and a golden sash that ends in violet. His hair shines much like the sun; it is shoulder length and curled at the end. He is a youthful twenty to twenty-two at the most. His smile is broad and warm. His eyes are set far apart and they appear to be blue, violet, and gold. They seem to have all of these qualities. His radiance shines as though he is enamored of everything, even this question!

Response: "Thank you for indulging me, Dear one. I know that this seems like an odd request."

EIGHTH JURISDICTION: CHARITY

His face is rather elongated, with a square jaw and high cheekbones, and a very sharp nose feature. His jaw is square but his chin is a bit rounded, his lips the color of a pink rose. They also have a golden quality to them, even in the pinkness. He is, in this instance, a full 6 foot 4 inches. when he stands, and he is definitely perfectly proportioned, like the Grecian Gods, whose musculature is perfected and balanced. He is the embodiment of an ideal. He truly is this, and he is giggling about the whole thing! In fact everyone is laughing at it. I'm still seated here, and they are all standing and chuckling! That we are concerned with such vanities as the personal appearance. It really is just the expression of perfected love as opposed to a vanity . . . so it's rather funny to them.

If you choose, we can proceed.

Response: "Thank you Dear one, you have been most patient."

Whichever you choose to express in Mastery comes through your desire to be of Service, and the greater your Service, the more complete your expression can be. We will proceed with Charity.

As he opens the book, he becomes his distinguished self again. He is opening the book to page numbered 332, which reads, "The Eighth Jurisdiction for the Province."

CHARITY IS THE EQUALIZER OF INJUSTICE AND INEQUITY

Charity.

Charity is that expression of the heart which is joy! It comes on the A sound. It comes on the beginning of the vowel frequencies.

Charity, those who give.

Charity, those who share.

Charity, those who allow the free flow of energy.

Charity, those who see balance in the expression of giving.

Those who seek nothing in reward are of Charity.

Charity is the free flow of energy from one to another. It comes from the heart's desire to Love and it is an expression of Service. It grows from this Service, but it is a type of Service. Charity gives all and expects nothing. From Charity comes the unboundness that is recognized by the loving heart.

Charity is a distribution, and it is the equalizer when there is unjustice and inequity. It is the expansive energy that clarifies all giving of the heart. It comes from what you would call, "gifts." Charity in its simplest form is a gift, as when one gives a gift and expects nothing in return. It is in this charitable gift giving that one finds joy in the delight of the recipient. It is given without thought of the delight of self but with the focus of the recipient coming to the ecstasy of the exchange. This energetic pattern has many, many times, in your world, been given with, as you would call it, strings attached. But a true gift has none of these. It is only a gift. It is the expression of joy because of the aboundness that exists in the universe.

GIVE WITHOUT DESIRE OF RETURN

This Abundance is for all to partake of and has always been a joy that we all have and are able to share. This joy and this gift are brought forth through charitable expression, the A sound. In your world, Charity has been mistaken as gift giving only. Is not a gift a gift of what you have? Whether it is your time, whether it is your counsel, whether it is your Love. Whether it is your money, whether it is your personal posessions or belongings, is not the sharing of these a charitable energetic pattern? Is not the giving of these, without want or desire of return, a charitable energetic pattern?

You all have the ability to be in this energetic pattern of Charity, no matter how you perceive yourself. Whether you perceive yourself as great or small, Charity is an eternal energetic flow. It is an exchange. It is how Service is manifest! Charity is an expression of Love!

Response: "I understand, Dear one. Thank you for reminding me of the joy which comes in this work! I realize how we forget that so easily."

THE JOY OF GIVING

Many times when we come to you to express, when we come to you to give Service, it is on the A vowel frequency sound. The Frequency of Charity! It is most joyous to give what we are! It is most joyous to give what we are to those who choose to receive! Many, many ask for reception, but do not choose to receive. We come to the hearts of many of humankind, the hearts that function just as ours function, and we ask, "Will you receive this? Will you allow us to be of service? Will you allow us to share? Can the Charity that exists in the universe be brought forth to you?"

Many say, "No." But many do say, "YES!" It is as the choice is. Charity flows in the allowance of the recipient. The recipient cooperates and says, "Yes, I would be most happy and gracious to receive this gift!" The joy of the recipient is the joy in the Charity! Here is the wellspring of all joy! It is in the giving. It is in the sharing and the allowing of the free exchange. Charity is what we all desire most to partake of. We all desire to have this expression. All in the universe choose Charity as a form of joy. It is the essence of joy!

This is a short discourse. It is a short Jurisdiction for this planet. And yet, it is a basic that Cooperation is allowed to become, this joy of Charity.

Response: "Thank you, Beloved."

Then we shall take our retirement from you now. I AM Sanat Kumara. You Dear one, are a child of my own heart.

EIGHTH JURISDICTION: CHARITY

You are the joy of Charity that I have been permitted to bring forth to your world. I thank you!

Response: "I thank you."

CHAPTER THIRTY-FOUR
Saint Germain and Sanat Kumara present the Ninth Jurisdiction

Desire

The Heart's Desire is the Source of Creation

*"Desire springs not only from the heart;
it comes from the soul, the spark of creativity."*
- SANAT KUMARA

Welcome Beloved chelas. I AM Saint Germain, Chohan of the Seventh Ray. And as you know, it is the Violet Flame that I have brought to this planet, and particularly for this Time of Transition. It is our hope that you will use it at least three times per day. For you see Dear one, it is what accelerates the metabolic rate of the system and allows one to access fourth alignment density.

I have stepped forth to escort you both to the Council table. Come Dear Brother and Sister. Come, Dear ones.

He is reaching his hand out to both of us. We are walking up pink and green marble stairs. We are walking up to the platform.

Dear ones, we ask for you to wait. Stand here. I shall summon the others.

Before us is the table and four pillars of light come forth. To the right side steps Saint Germain and to the left, Archangel Michael. Sitting at the table is Beloved Sanat Kumara. Behind him stands Beloved Sananda, accompanied by six angels.

Step forward, Dear children. I AM Sanat Kumara. As you are here, I assume you have given your permission for us to proceed with discourse. Is this so?

Response: "Please proceed."

You have been brought here so we may dispense the Ninth Jurisdiction for the Province, as read from the Golden Leafed Books. You see, Dear ones, these Jurisdictions are the structure or law that your planet has been built upon. There are Universal Laws and there are Cosmic Laws. Universal Laws are, basically, foundation law; they are consistent wherever one goes. Cosmic law is built upon the principles of Universal Law; however, Cosmic Law will vary. Cosmic Law varies from planet to planet, solar system to solar system, and is specific. In this instance, these Jurisdictions are specifically for this Province.

Now Michael is handing him the book and streams of violet and streams of blue are crossing in front of him. He lays the book exactly where these Rays cross. The letters on this book are gold. He reads,

Jurisdictions for the Province.

He is turning the pages.

THE IMAGE AND LIKENESS OF A CREATOR

Jurisdiction Number Nine: Desire.

Desire springs not only from the heart, it comes from the soul, the spark of creativity. Upon your planet it was decided that these beings should be creative beings, so they were made in the image and likeness of a Creator.

But what would assure that these beings would carry this code within them? And so the Spark of Desire was planted within them. At first, it was planted as a Threefold Flame within the heart of man. This flame represented Love, Wisdom, and Power, and the flame was identified with the Pink Ray, the Yellow Ray, and the Blue Ray. There was a time upon your planet when the flame was held not only in the heart but within the entire structure of the energetic body. From head to toe, this flame spanned. The Desire among the mass was to express creativity.

Great works of creation flourished upon your planet, not only works of beauty and art, but also great works of genetic engineering, and great works that expanded beyond this solar system. This Law of Desire was planted within, and is what you may refer to as a genetic code. It is a Great Spark that identifies the Creator's creations.

Let us identify Desire. Before the days of forgetting, the Great Spark of Desire was all that there was. It circulated through the flame in a continuous circular motion. The bodies that held it never required an intake of food. Do you understand?

The bodies held continuous Desire within them. The flame that was held was fanned continuously, for one not only knew his source, he realized that he was a source! For he was made in the image and likeness of the Father/Mother, the Mighty I AM Presence. The spark which was held was within the Heart of Desire.

THE INNATE FLAME

As collective forgetting spread across the face of the planet and the light decreased, a balance of night and day came. The bodies required rest in the hours of darkness, and the great Threefold Flame seated itself in a place of protection, a safe harbor called the heart. It has been held here for many centuries. Its recognition is now to become part of this great period of Grace!

Desire in earlier ages has been identified as hope. Hope is the light at the edge of darkness which assures that the light shall return again. It is the ember which carries the light of the flame during the period of darkness, to the period of light. It was recognized that this ember was held during this period of darkness and you know now that this period is only that of nightfall.

The flame's source of renewal must be protected! The ember was encased by a circular motion from the energetic combination of the solar plexus and the heart. These two forces combined to form a protective shell around this flame. A protective shell held the flame through night. Great Angels came to hold and create a space of protection, for they realized that during this time of darkness the ember seed could indeed disintegrate. And so hope was born!

Hope is indeed a sound vibration, built upon what you now know as the OM. It protects the Flame of Desire, the genetic and cellular blueprint within the heart, the flame that links Creator to creation, parent to child.

BLUEPRINT OF CREATIVITY: THE SOURCE

We have explored the origin of hope and Desire as a scientific energetic. It is no mystery to those upon your planet that you carry a blueprint as an inheritor of this kingdom. But how does this concept of Desire fit within your world today? There is the Desire of the Heart. There is the Desire of the Mind. The Desire of the Heart is the Desire of creativity! The Desire of the Mind is how you hold your focus. Creativity, focus, and the Desire of the Heart combine together to form the energetic layer called the ninth body. You have held this ninth energetic body before Dear ones! And it is coming back to you!

In your Piscean era, hope and Desire were held as mysterious concepts. People felt if they hoped enough, the end result would happen. People felt if they desired enough, the end result would happen. Dear ones, Desire is the natural blueprint that you carry. It is not passion. It is empassioned. It is not hope, but it is hopeful! Dear ones, Desire is your source! Without it you could not be. It is that simple. It is the seed. It is the spark. It is the source of origin. It is scientific and it is melodic.

It is the beginning, Dear ones, and, in a sense, yes, it is the end. For without Desire, you can hold nothing. Its Divine Complement is focus. Remember, Dear ones, to Desire without focus is to build without a foundation! Remember they work hand in hand together, Brother with Brother, Sister with Sister. There will come a time upon your planet when Desire will not be held, but carried within each cell of your being. For it is indeed the source of enlightenment. We invite you to join us through Desire!

THE OM VIBRATION

Question: "Thank you. Does the OM vibration protect the Flame of Desire?"

It is the O. You complete the cycle with the M. However, it's purest form, as sung by the angels, is the O. We have included the M to bring it to full circle. The vibration then grounds to your planet and is protected.

Response: "I understand."

The O runs throughout the human physiology. Each of these sounds given to you opens up particular meridians that allow access through the energy locations in the energetic field to dimensional expression.

Question: "I understand. Now with Desire, what sound is this?"

Hope is the O. Desire is the combination of the U and the O.

Question: "Does the U precede the O?"

The O precedes the U.

Question: "So if I were to intone, OOOOUUUU, would this be correct?"

That is accurate Dear one, does not that sound a 3/4 and the beat of your heart?

Response: "Yes, it fills the entire body."

It is the energetic frequency to increase the flame about your body and to become a source for all of your selves.

A SPIRITUAL POLARITY OF LIGHT AND DARK

Question: "At the time when there was only light on this planet, all of the continents were a disk?"

They were a continuous circle.

Question: "And did our North Pole protrude through the center of this circle to align to the sun?"

The land floated continuously on the face of waters.

Question: "So, as the Earth rotated on its axis, the continents moved in the water always to be aligned with the sun?"

This is correct.

Question: "So the axis did not protrude through this continuous circle of land mass?"

No, it did not. You are experiencing a planet which has become fixed and rigid, and has a difficult time with energy movement.

Question: "When the doubt of divinity came into our minds, was this when the continents becamed fixed and rigid?"

NINTH JURISDICTION: DESIRE

This was a slow process, Dear one. As the movement became more fixed, mankind experienced nightfall, at first at short spans. And then a time fell upon the planet when her darkness was held in greater esteem than light! Do you understand your energetic body and its relationship to light?

Response: "Without the light there is no movement, expansion, growth, or creativity."

You have begun to understand, Dear one. Do you have more questions?

Question: "The moment of doubt, was this brought about as a test?"

It energetically burst within the cellular structure. Do you understand?

Question: "Yes. Who instigated the moment of doubt?"

Those who chose to test the coloration of black.

Response: "Oh! Black exists in creation in the negative dimensions"

It does indeed, Dear one.

Question: "For that is the balance?"

It does indeed show contrast and does indeed, at times, give balance. However, it was declared that, in this universe, black would not be contained within the cellular structure of this creation. And it is not contained within the Threefold Flame.

Question: "Was it the Archangel Satan, who pulled the dimension of negativity through to the positive?"

He asked to experiment with the Black Ray, knowing full well that the genetic and cellular structure would not hold it! It has been an experiment and it is obvious that it does not work.

Question: "Has this been an example for the rest of creation?"

Dear one, it was known before not to mix vibration.

Response: "Yes."

The colors of your universe are of the lighter variety. Their intensity has a pitch, as you call it. The pitch is formed on 144,000 revolutions per millisecond.

Dear one, I must take my leave, if there are no further questions.

Response: "I see it is that time, and I thank you very much for your patience and for your teaching."

Beloved Saint Germain shall escort you.

Response: "It has been a joy to be in your presence."

AND I LOVE YOU DEAR ONES. I AM THE LIGHT AND SOUND OF THE UNIVERSE.

Response: "Thank you."

Saint Germain now escorts us.

Welcome Beloveds. I AM Saint Germain. Take my hand. As we walk, we shall discourse with you regarding this. This has been a most important teaching, as you can see.

Response: "Yes. I truly hope my questions are not inappropriate. "

They were not Dear ones. It took the great resonation of Beloved Sanat Kumara to come and give this to you!

Response: "*Yes.*"

We would like this information to go forth. For it is to stream forth for the Illumination of the minds of humankind!

Response: "I understand. I do agree to this."

Thank you, Dear one. I bless you and hold you in the heart of the Violet Flame! Your Brother and co-worker, I AM Saint Germain.

CHAPTER THIRTY-FIVE
Saint Germain and Sananda
present the Tenth Jurisdiction

Faith

Trust Your Creative Birthright

*"Faith is the agreement between the focus of
your desire and the stillness of creation."*
- SANANDA

Welcome Beloved chelas! I AM your Brother, Saint Germain. Take my hand and walk with me. Dear ones, again I must ask for permission to enter your energy field. I apologize for assuming such.

Response: "You have my constant and unending permission to enter my field. I love you."

Walk with me down this corridor.

We are blending together as we each take his hand. I have his left, Len his right. And we're walking down the hall that has filtered green light. We're coming to a large arched door, a double golden door. There are symbols on this door.

Dear one, before we enter the chamber, it is my request that you record the location of where we are.

THE DOOR OF SYMBOLS

Response: "Please proceed, Dear one."

We have entered into the space that exists between dimensions. It is in these spaces that exist between all dimensions that function is determined. In each of these spaces, creation has stepped forth to serve in beauty and majestic splendor! These doors in front of you, the golden doors to the Chamber of the Council, contain on it symbols. Look closely, and you shall see the symbols of twelve tribes!

I look and can clearly see six. Saint Germain begins to identify the six.

To name a few of these. Observe these, Dear ones, for they all have been part of your Earth history. It was decided that from this space that Jurisdictions should come forth. They are given to determine the shape of the 1,000 year period.

We have spoken to you of geometric languages, and these Jurisdictions are founded upon the geometric language of your universe.

A trumpet sounds. Do you hear Dear ones?

It sounds like a thousand trumpets.

The doors are open and we may enter. Take my hands Dear ones, and we shall walk up these stairs.

TENTH JURISDICTION: FAITH

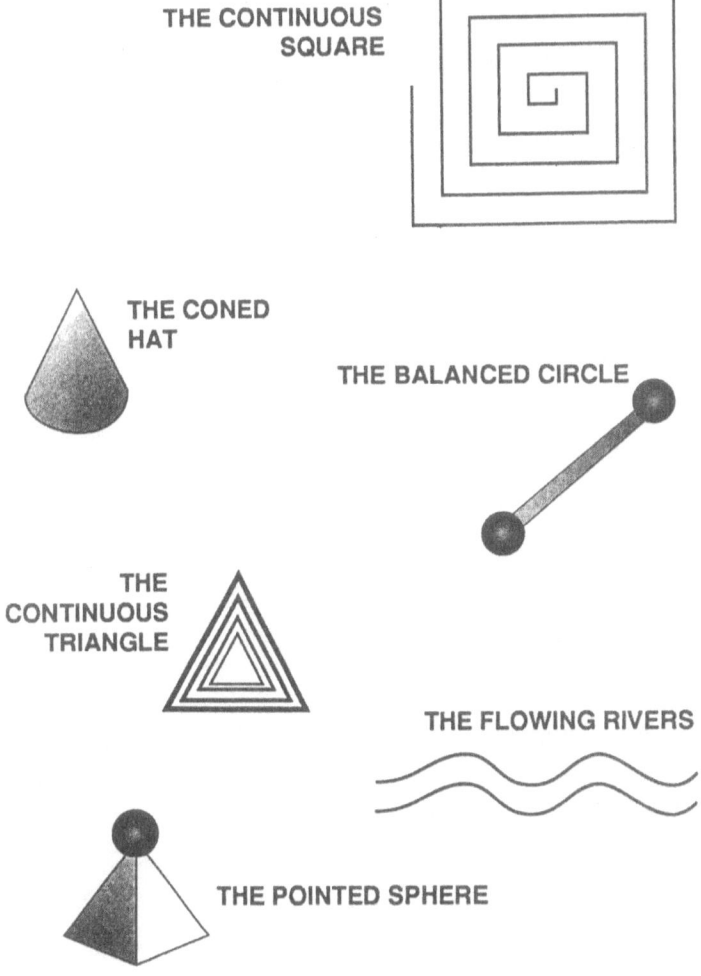

(ABOVE) *Six Symbols from the Golden Doors of the Chamber of Planetary Justice*

We are walking up stairs that are milky green in color. Twelve steps, and come to a podium and the table.

Dear ones, take your chairs, and I shall take my stance behind Beloved Sananda, Brother and Comrade of the Twelfth Ray!

Sananda is seated at the table. Behind him is Saint Germain, to his right, Archangel Michael, and to his left is Archangel Chamuel. Two Rays focus in front of him and the book densifies.

Welcome, my Beloved students and children. Do we have permission to read this Jurisdiction to you?

Response: "Please read this Jurisdiction."

FAITH IS "KNOWING"

Jurisdiction Number Ten: Faith.

In the stillness, before creation stepped forth across your planet, there was that moment, we refer to as a space of stillness, where one could doubt. At this moment, the Rays and their pulsations stopped. It is a split second in time, or, as you would say, in the event, a split second where the Rays mix together to see this form they have brought forth. What is the energy that would bond this together? The continuous motion that we have spoken of, Faith!

TENTH JURISDICTION: FAITH

Faith is an expansive energy and held in continual form. Its birth is, too, of Desire, but its desire used as expansion. Faith is the moment before stillness. Faith is the moment where one again chooses to continue the desire of focus or not. It is said by wise men, "to be or not to be." What is being spoken of is Faith, to choose or not to choose, to hold or not to hold. Faith is carried by each of the Beloved Rays. They have recognized that without Faith, the light they carry will not expand. For you to create, Dear ones, and to achieve anything within your being, Faith is, indeed, an essential ingredient.

Faith is the agreement between the focus of your desire and the stillness of creation. Faith is the light that is seen long before you have eyes to see! Faith is the ability to carry on when one has no strength. Faith is a reserved energetic and held, as you would say, in a space between a space.

In all plans created which then stream forth, we understand their ability to be is a choice of free will. Faith is what comes forth to allow a pattern to be. The changing winds blow upon your planet, and it is Faith that allows form to come forth through change! It has been said that when a plan fails, another shall emerge. What allows the plan to go forth? The pivot point called Faith. For your times, Dear ones, upon your planet, one may be caught in the perils of transition; it is therefore important you carry the key of Faith!

Beloved ones, from the Keys of Peter, Faith is known as the tonal A. It allows the collective thought to be gathered and aligns the wills of humanity to that of the heavenly host. Light is then breathed with direction!

Faith is an expression of the Law of Love. It is expanded and carried throughout your world by those who know that Faith is a choice for creation. Keep your Faith, Dear ones. Do not hide it or lock it away! It is yours and your birthright. It was given to you by the Mighty I AM THAT I AM.

Faith has been brought forth to bond creation. Remember, in the stillness of the Rays they all carry Faith.

He is closing the book, and standing up.

AS YOU HAVE EYES TO SEE AND EARS TO HEAR, KNOW THAT I AM SANANDA! AND KNOW THAT IT WAS FAITH THAT BROUGHT ME HERE AND KEPT ME HERE! ALMIGHTY I AM, FAITH!

CHAPTER THIRTY-SIX
Sanat Kumara presents the
Eleventh Jurisdiction

Stillness

The Law of Alignment

*"Stillness is the space where energy is gathered
and aligned to come forth in a manifestation."*
- SANAT KUMARA

We are standing at a great archway. It is marble, colored pink and green, and we are proceeding down a great green corridor. On either side there are additional archways.

We are coming to these great arched doors. These are massive gold doors that contain many symbols of many geometrical languages. The doors are now opening wide. A set of stairs is before us and in front of us are Saint Germain, Sananda, and Archangel Michael. We are following behind the three of them. We ascend the stairs to the platform and come to the room of green and pink marble. We are approaching a desk and seated there is Sanat Kumara. To Sanat Kumara's right is Saint Germain, to Sanat Kumara's left is Archangel Michael. And off to the right behind Sanat Kumara, standing, is Sananda. There is a great opening behind them through which gold light is streaming. We are coming once again to the book.

Greetings Beloved children of the Golden Light. I AM Sanat Kumara.

Response: "Greetings Beloved Dear one."

I ask you to come forth much closer, and I ask your permission to enter into your energy.

Response: "We give our permission."

You will notice there are three chairs. Please be seated.

Response: "Thank you."

We are now at the Eleventh Jurisdiction for the Province. This is the Jurisdiction of Stillness. Before I commence, we shall proceed with examples of Stillness within your world.

There is a Stillness always at your sunrise and your sunset. There is a Stillness always before there is a storm. There is a Stillness always before a volcanic eruption. There is a Stillness always before you have an earthquake. There is a Stillness always just before the birth of any creature of creation! There is a soft Stillness just before energy changes, or before new creation comes forth.

STILLNESS GATHERS AND ALIGNS ENERGIES

Stillness.

This is a Law of Creation, for the Stillness is the space where the energies are gathered and aligned to come forth in a manifestation. It is in the Stillness of your thought, your quiet contemplation that you offer yourself of Service. It is the Stillness before you perform any act of great contribution to creation. In this space is the allowance for creation. It is the allowance that comes forth for each of you to choose.

For in that Stillness, Mother Earth will choose to erupt or not. It is in that Stillness that the storm can choose to come forth with great power and great precision.

It is in the Stillness that the Earth finds a completed cycle. It is at times, as you say, to catch your breath; to catch your breath in thought; to catch your breath in emotion.

This Stillness is in all creation! It is between the atoms of your existence. It is between the Rays of creation. There exists the Stillness! It is between the densities. It is between the universes. There is even a Stillness between each of your energy bodies. It is a point of transition, and it is a point where you may contemplate and choose. It serves as a functional space that is carried through allowing. It serves as a function to focus. It is in the moment of the I AM. The I AM is the completion in all the Stillness. The I AM is the function in all the Stillness. The I AM is the comprehension of all that is still.

THE REVITALIZING BREATH

You have come forth and offered yourself in Service. Before your choice of Service you found a Stillness. You found a Stillness where you found your I AM, where you found your own divinity. And from that point all choice that is aligned with the Divine is made. So stillness is, my Dear ones, the point of aligning with the Divine Choice. It is the space that gives you breath when you find yourself weary. It is the space that is always there in support of you. It asks nothing and gives all. It is in this space that your Creatorship comes forth! It is in this space that the greatness of your divinity is manifest!

Question: "This is most beautiful, Dear one. I ask that you clarify, I AM THAT I AM, could that be representative of the space of stillness?"

It is indeed Dear one. You have found the key. I AM THAT I AM is the energetic pattern of the stillness that is in all creation.

Question: "The A tonation that is used in the word *that* is the specific tonal formula, is this so?"

SILENCE IS GOLDEN

Yes. It is AAA. Does this not refer back to Creator Apollo? Does this not refer back to Athena, Mother Creator? Does this A not refer back to that frequency that is the structure of all the universe? For it is their radiance that comes in the Stillness. You have seen Stillness and silence as darkness, but you see, silence, my Dear one, is golden! Has not silence been called Golden? It is the stillness that is Golden, that streams forth from the Heart of Great Apollo. I AM THAT I AM. Do you have further questions?

Question: "Yes I do. So in this Stillness, is this also the point of creation that bonds in the intake of breath and the exhale of breath?"

Breath is the cycle of creation that comes forth. Breath is the allowance of you moving into your Stillness. For eons in many monasteries, was it not in the breath that each sat within their Stillness, and continuously cycled that within? In the Stillness, the breath allows the flow from within you.

Question: "So Stillness is an ever-giving power that is self-generating?"

Stillness is an ever-giving power that is generated from the I AM THAT I AM. And, if you see the Source within you, then you see the self as the Source. Because in seeing the Source, you have chosen to come Home!

Question: "Becoming still can sometimes be difficult. Is there a way for stillness to come more quickly?"

STEP OUT OF SELF

Stillness is a focus; it is a choice. Step out of yourself for the moment, even though there is, what you call, noise or disturbance. Feel the Stillness of the rock. Feel the Stillness of the air. Feel the gentle ring that Stillness is. Feel the Stillness without you; find that and you may breathe it in.

Response: "Thank you, Dear one. I am most honored to be in your presence."

It is I, Dear one, who is honored to be in your presence for your Service with all of us. We are complete in our Service to you. I AM Sanat Kumara.

Question: "Thank you Dear one, and who shall come forth for Creativity?"

Dear one, Creativity will be brought forth by your immediate parents, for they have brought you forth. They have breathed you out in this Service so that you have come forth in our family! They will bring forth this Service to you as you bring forth your Service to them.

Response: "Thank you Dear one. I understand."

I AM Sanat Kumara. I AM THE LOVE OF GOD THAT NEVER FAILS TO ALIGN THE WILL TO THE DIVINE!

CHAPTER THIRTY-SEVEN
Saint Germain, Apollo, and Mother Mary
present the Twelfth Jurisdiction

Creation

Part One: The Law of Divine Order

*"Creation! See it pulse with the sweetness of life!
The joy of giving the Law of Love."*
- MOTHER MARY

Beloved Mighty I AM Presence, Great Host of Ascended Masters of the Spiritual Hierarchy of the Great White Brotherhood. To Beloved Mother Mary, Beloved Sananda, Beloved Sanat Kumara, Lady Master Venus, Beloved Saint Germain, Beloved Portia, Beloved Kuan Yin, Beloved El Morya, Beloved Kuthumi, come forth Dear ones. I give you permission to enter my energy fields. I align my will with the Divine Will, and ask to bring forth this work in the greatest clarity to serve the planet.

Holy, holy, holy, Lord God of Hosts. I ask for the Beloved Brothers and Sisters of the White Brotherhood to come forth on this day to bring forth the Twelfth Jurisdiction, that of Creation and Creativity. Come forth into my field!

Welcome my Beloved chelas and Beloved students of the Light of God that Never Fails. I AM Saint Germain and I come forth on the Violet Ray of Mercy, Forgiveness, and Compassion, which is the Violet Transmuting Ray for the one thousand year period of Grace that will be bestowed upon your planet, Dear ones. Do I have permission to enter your energy field?

Response: "Please come forth into my energy field."

I come forth and offer myself as the bridge! You see, Dear ones, I truly am what you call a bridge to freedom. I AM a bridge which has been offered for this transitional age. I bridge myself to you Dear ones, to bring you to the Planetary Council of Justice. Take my hands Dear ones, and we shall walk down the hallway.

Before we start, Dear ones, I ask you to put these robes on.

He is offering us these white robes. Gold is on all the edges of the garment.

Dear ones, please slip on what we call the seamless garment! You see, Dear ones, the seamless garment signifies purity of intent and desire, and that you stepped forth with an intent of innocence and purity in the Desire for Service.

Take my hand now and walk with me.

Len has his right hand, and I his left hand, and we are walking down a hall filled with misty light. A pink light coming from the walls surrounds us in a cloud of pink. We are coming to the doorway, the door of symbols.

A knock sounds on the door three times. The doors open and a voice booms,

"Enter, Beloved Children of the Golden Sun!"

We are walking up the stairway bathed in the brilliant light of this sun. The light of Apollo shines!

We continue to walk up the steps, twelve steps to be exact. Each stair is lined with gold. We come to the podium and the desk. At the Council sit Beloved Apollo, Beloved Sanat Kumara, Beloved Kuan Yin, Portia, El Morya, Kuthumi, Soltec, Archangel Michael, Archangel Gabriel, Archangel Jophiel, Archangel Chamuel, Archangel Raphael, Archangel Zadkiel and Archangel Uriel!

The Seven Archangels are standing in a line at the back, each representing one of the Seven Rays. This great host of Ascended Beings are all standing before us as we walk, and they are applauding for us!

THE RESTORATION OF EARTH

Apollo steps forward.

My Beloved children, it is with great joy that we welcome you to this Council of Planetary Justice. This work that comes forth is the last of the Twelve Jurisdictions for the Province and for your planet, which we restore as Prahna.

Dear ones, it was the continuous Light that Never Failed that brought forth the continuous Breath that Never Failed. We ask for you to breathe into this 1,000 year period of Grace, this transition that comes forth upon your planet Prahna. We ask for you to bring this information in the highest light of Clarity, so all may see it for what it is! The eternal truth is the Light and Breath of God that Never Fails! For this is universal and built upon the Law of Love. Never again shall your planet fail after the sustaining period of 1,000 years.

We applaud your effort, Dear ones! We applaud your effort for what you have brought forth to the planet! We realize the tremendous focus of Desire needed for this to come forth and be individualized on your planet! And you, who have been appointed for this work of the Eighth Ray, the Golden Ray, I give you the quality, DESIRE! For this is what you have individualized and brought to this planet!

Desire is a quality of the Eighth Ray. It has been brought forth in an illumined Desire. It has been brought forth in a clear Desire. It has been brought forth in the strength of Desire. Do you see, Dear ones, this work you have brought to the planet? And it is we who applaud you . . . for each of us has individualized, as you must too!

STAND AS A CO-CREATOR

These Twelve Jurisdictions that come forth are Jurisdictions that set the stage for the Eighth Ray! For the maintenance and sustaining of the period of Harmony, so that these laws shall come forth. Dear ones, I AM a Creator of your universe, and again, I have a Source that created me! Stand not in awe of me, but stand as a Co-creator, next to my heart.

Yes, it was I who sponsored this Star seed. And it was I who breathed out from my lips the Desire of the Law of Love! But I ask of you, as I stand here applauding your effort, and also the end result of your work, that you stand, not in awe of me, but stand shoulder to shoulder, one among me! Comrade to comrade, Brother to Brother, Sister to Sister. Dear ones, I AM Apollo, and I honor your work. Step forth, Dear ones, as we welcome you as a member to the Council.

Now from his ring finger, he removes a ring with an insignia of the sun. Twelve perfect Rays stream from the round circle.

Dear one, I ask for you to wear my ring.

Response: "I accept."

He is now asking Len to hold out his ring finger. He now places the gold band displaying the sun symbol. He then turns to me.

Dear one, it is indeed the Desire of your heart that this has sprung forth! And from my heart, I give to you my sign.

Another ring appears on his ring finger. On it is not the Threefold Flame, but a Fourfold Flame!

I hold out my hand and he places the ring of the Fourfold Flame on my finger.

Dear ones, these symbols have been brought to you, not as a source of forgetting or a source of remembering, but they have been brought to you to honor the work that you have brought to Prahna.

Dear ones, I step back, and leave your frequency. I AM Apollo! And I practice the LAW OF LOVE at all times. HITAKA. HITAKA. HITAKA!

Saint Germain is coming forward.

Dear ones, I present you a chair.

Two chairs are presented by angels and we both sit down.

And now Beloved Mary comes to the center of the table and sits. Beloved Archangel Raphael stands behind her, to her right is Sananda, and to her left is Kuan Yin.

The Archangels now have departed but they have left a legion of Seraphim and Cherubim. They are all holding hands in a ringed circle, above us and below us.

Welcome my Beloved children. From the Desire of the heart, I AM Mary, and request your permission to enter your energy field.

Response: "Please come forward, Mary."

THE CYCLE OF ONE

Dear ones, I have been asked to read Jurisdiction Twelve, the part known for the planet Prahna, Creation.

A Green Ray and a Gold Ray come forth. Together they weave in front of her and the book appears! She opens to the latter part of the book and to the gold letters, Creation.

It is indeed the Desire of the heart that Creation comes forth. From the lips of the Creator of Creators came the words "LET THERE BE LIGHT!" And the angels of sound carried out this command! What was welled within the heart of the Creator before? Even the sound provoked the action. Desire!

You have a Law of Desire upon your planet, Dear ones, but now we shall look at Creation and the sweetness of Desire.

The Law of Love mixes as a symphony with Desire, and Creation comes forth. Creation comes from the pure, clean heart that joyously accepts whatever form steps forth.

Creation is from the inner Desire to be as ONE with the universe. Creation comes from what is indeed, the sweetness of the smile. For this is the reflection of the innocence of Creation. Creation is a being that carries within it a consciousness that is unique unto itself. And from this uniqueness sprang twelve individual Rays!

Creation is a Source, indeed, and as a self-perpetuating motion, it pulses with the Desire within. Radiating from this Source of Creation are the Twelve Rays.

Upon your planet Creation has expressed itself as Seven Rays. The Eighth Ray steps forward, Dear ones so you will understand. I AM Mary, the Beloved Mother and sponsor for this Eighth Ray coming forth.

Creation is, too, a cycle. It recognizes when something has completed and that another should step forward. As we prepare to complete our cycle, we must assure, as Creators, that Creation continues on! To fashion within the heart a Flame of Desire, Love, Wisdom, and Power is honored as well.

Creation is a trust. Do you not see Dear ones? Creation is the trust that all shall continue on and on. It is, indeed, a rhythmic expansion. For it is the thought of trust that allows Divine Order to continue. It is the thought of faith that allows this trust to continue. It is the thought, yes, of hope that allows this trust to continue.

Upon your planet there have been many hours of darkness. But we rejoice in the many hours of light! And the many hours of light yet to come! For this great light to stream forth upon your planet, the planet Prahna, which will express the effervescent, everlasting foundation of Creation! The Light of God that Never Fails!

TWELFTH JURISDICTION: CREATION

Dear ones, Creation is the Source, and Creation is the expansion. Creation is the rhythm and the orderliness and the timeliness. Creation contains within it also the Law of Love. Beyond the Law of Love, is the Desire of the heart. Beyond the Desire of the heart, is the sweetness of being!

To express Creation, Dear ones, is really to be what you are, all that you are, and all that you have been given.

Creation is divine and sacred. It is, too, a continual breath, but we ask for you to see Creation as a continuous flame.

Creation contains within it many segments that comprise the whole. Stand back Dear ones, and observe the whole. See this magnificent piece of art! Creation! See it pulse with the sweetness of life! The joy of giving the Law of Love!

You have been brought forth in Creation to express joy!

She is turning the page. And there are only a few words on the page.

Life is the Eternal Creation.

On the next page,

Amen, Amen, Amen. Grace bestowed upon Prahna! Amen, Amen, Amen!

Dear ones, may I be of Service to you?

Question: "Does this complete?"

This completes what you know as Creation.

Response: "I understand. It is perfect as it is."

We thank you and love you, Dear ones, and take our rest.

ETERNALLY YOURS, FROM THE HEART OF DESIRE, THE LAW OF LOVE, LIFE EVERLASTING, COMPLETE WITH GRACE, CREATION, I AM MARY.

A trumpet sounds and the ring of angels opens the circle. A great light appears and in this light the book is carried up and dissipates. Saint Germain steps forward.

Dear ones, we thank you for your work of Service. I shall send two Violet Flame Angels to assist you.

The two angels escort us down the stairs, through the doors, and remove our robes. We see each other and our eyes are gold! Our hair is gold! Our hands are cupped to each other, and a gold beam appears for us to travel back to our Earthly bodies.

CHAPTER THIRTY-SEVEN
Saint Germain, Apollo, and Sananda present the Twelfth Jurisdiction

Creativity

Part Two: The Law of Divine Order

"Creation is ONE. Creativity is part of!"
- SANAT KUMARA

Beloved Saint Germain, Beloved Mother Mary, Beloved Kuthumi, Beloved El Morya, Beloved Sanat Kumara, Beloved Kuan Yin, Portia, Lady Master Venus, and all hosts of Ascended Masters, all Archangels and all angels of the Angelic Realm. Cherubim, Seraphim, Powers, Dominions and Glories. All Elohim and Chohans of each Ray. Come forth in this moment so we may complete this Twelfth Jurisdiction. Dear ones, come forth into our energy fields. I ask, for I am of Service to you.

There is a great green light, and the great green light contains pink light, gold light, and also blue light. There is once again the hallway that we have traveled down before. Len and I are going together. I AM at his right side. We are coming to this great door that carries all of these geometric shapes.

The doors are opening and I see Saint Germain accompanied by several angels.

He is motioning and he says:

Greetings Beloved Children of the Golden Flame. I AM Saint Germain!

We are stopping there at the door, and we are once again enrobed.

Response: "Greetings Beloved Saint Germain. Thank you for your patience."

Dear Child of the Golden Light, it is your patience and persistence that we thank, for we do understand that in your world of thought and feeling, much transpires in your moment to moment experiences.

We are now robed. We're moving forward, once again holding Saint Germain's hands as we ascend the steps, the same golden steps as yesterday. As we come to the top there are great hosts of angels around us. There is also great music and song! There is joy and sounds of trumpets and harps. There are choirs and choirs of angels, all singing.

PRAISE TO THE MOST HIGH! PRAISE TO THE LIGHT OF ALL LIGHT! PRAISE AND GLORY IN THE ETERNAL WONDERMENT OF THE CREATOR OF CREATORS!

We are coming forward once again, and the Council is convening, leaving one space. There is a chair missing in the center, replaced by a great gold and pink light!

TWELFTH JURISDICTION: CREATIVITY

We are standing in front of the Council, and Apollo enters!

Response: "Greetings Beloved Apollo."

Greetings Dear children of the Golden Light! Welcome, and come forward to this table and Council.

We are moving forward to the table. In each of his hands is a golden wreath of laurel. He is placing them on our heads. He is seated now and we are also seated.

We greet Apollo with our right hands over our hearts. All the other Ascended Ones do the same, and all the faces are beaming with smiles.

Come forward Dear ones. Be seated. In this moment of VICTORY we place the Laurel of Gratitude upon you! It is our heart's longing pouring forth to you to complete this, so that Prahna may once again be the perfect glistening gem of Creation that she truly is!

Response: "It is my greatest Desire, I AM of Service."

This is noted and accepted, for you are the embodiment of Desire! You are the focus of the Desire of Creation! You are the perfection of Desire! And it is we, of this Council, who are thankful for your Desire. For this is the first step of Creation and the first step in the restoration of order. It is indeed this Desire! We ask you to hold this Desire, this flame, always within you!

He is extending his hands, and from each of his palms a Fourfold Flame arcs to each of our Heart Chakras. This flame is burning, totally kindled, and alight in each of us.

This is the Desire of Creation! This is the Desire of perfection! You are now of this perfection as you always have been. Recognize this in each other. Light this light in all you meet, for Desire is the first step in All That Is.

He is now standing up.

GLORY, GLORY, GLORY TO THE DESIRE OF Creation! For this truly is from the Creator of Creators.

Everyone is repeating with him,

GLORY, GLORY, GLORY TO THE DESIRE OF CREATION!
GLORY, GLORY, GLORY TO THE DESIRE OF CREATION!
GLORY, GLORY, GLORY TO THE DESIRE OF CREATION!

He is now taking leave from us. He is becoming again the gold light that shines behind everything.

Sananda, who was at Apollo's left side, is directly in front of us. The Angelic Realm is rising up behind him, the Archangels are the closest. There are eight Rays, four from each side of the long table, coming across and intersecting in a matrix. The book is precipitating through these Rays.

Greetings my Beloved children.

Response: "Greetings Dear Sananda."

I AM Sananda. You, whom I have held close to my heart since the first breath of your expression! You, who are of my light, and I AM of yours.

Response: "Thank you, Dear Father."

CREATIVITY IS THE "BECOMING"

You who are breath of my breath! Heart of my heart! You! I AM very pleased that you have continued on in the trade that we ply here of messengership. I AM very pleased that you hold the Desire of Completion! Now we come to the final step of references noted in this book for the Province, these Jurisdictions. We come to this final step so that all may understand Creativity! So that all may understand that the vibration of Creation comes forth from the Desire of Creativity!

This Creativity is the actual expression of active energy, the activated motion of Creation. For a thing of beauty that is set in a moment of perfection is indeed, in that moment, always in perfection! It is the becoming of the Creativity that is the motion that brings forth the Creation. This comes only from Desire. Creativity is the process and the path that all must follow to bring forth the perfection of Creation! It is the perfect Oneness, the eternal understanding that allows motion.

It is the becoming. It is the unfolding. It is the enfolding. It is the expansion. It is even the compaction of the motion of Creation! Creativity is the sum and total of all frequencies of Creation being expressed.

See Creativity as you sow the seed in the field. See Creativity as you carve the wood to fulfill your Desire, as you paint the picture, as you draw and design your buildings and machines. See Creativity in the words your write. See Creativity in the love you express!

See Creativity in the sports, the excelling of your bodies. All is the expression of Creation and each of these is a frequency of Creation. Each frequency is Creativity, and it is the collective Creativity that is the I AM of Creation.

He is now turning the page.

CREATION IS ONE, CREATIVITY IS PART OF

Creativity follows the natural law. It follows in the expressive Desire of the Oneness of Creation. Each expression of each lifestream is, in itself, Creativity. Each Desire in each one of you in your density is an expression of Creativity. Therefore each one plays a role and a part in the great symphony of Creation! For the Creation is the motion of all collective beings. Creativity is the E sound of the motion of the creative wave! It is on the e-motion that Creativity is expressed.

We have always hoped, for this planet Prahna, that Creativity, the e-motion, would be an accelerating point for all of Creation to expand. And it is our Desire that the expansion continue on from this point. That this e-motion, this Creativity, move forward in the expansion of the Oneness of this universe and of reflecting this Oneness back to the power and Creator of all Creators! For it is within each of us, in the perfection, the Oneness, the perfection that we are! The ONE perfected Cell, that you now realize exists! It is in this part of Creation that we are all joined to be creative. Reflect this back to your mighty I AM, and back further to the power of all powers.

He is turning the final pages.

THE LITURGY OF CO-CREATION

Blessed be Creation! Blessed be Creativity! Blessed be the ONE who is Creative and seeks no reward but only the expression of Creation!

Blessed is this creative energy, this Desire, blessed and loving from the heart and mind of our Father of fathers.

Glory and praise be to Creation! Glory and praise be to the Creative flow!

Glory and praise be to all who participate in this creative flow.

He turns the page again.

Amen, Amen, Amen. Creation is ONE! Creativity is part of.

Let this all be expressed in the Oneness.

Do you require any assistance?

Response: "Thank you, Dear Sananda. Almighty I AM, thank you for the source of all Creation, in which I too share. I find this Jurisdiction perfected."

Let this Jurisdiction and all preceeding go forth on the wings of Creation. Let these go forth for all the ages of humanity to hear, to know, and to be. Let the Perfected Cell of each member in this Creation resonate in the Oneness.

And if you have no further Desire, may we please take leave, creative one?

Response: "Thank you Beloved Father for all that you have given me. I AM in Service to the mighty I AM."

All that I AM is yours! There is no separation.

Question: "Is it you who sends the bluebird to my window?"

Always as a reminder, that you and the blue bird have a Oneness and a message. He who brings the message to you reflects the beauty of Creation to you! In your moments of doubt, come forward in a choice that is clear. Come forward in a choice that is known of your own divinity. Come forward in a choice and see your perfection and you will have no doubt. For I AM with you always. Never do I leave you! There is no separation.

Dear one, it is my wish that this work go forth, to not only the hearts and minds of man, but to lift the consciousness of man and his body to the Kingdom of I AM.

We thank you for your patience, and for your Desire. We will continue forward with the information for the rest of the Earth Changes.

We will now take leave of you.

Response: Thank you Sananda.

CHAPTER THIRTY-EIGHT
with Sanat Kumara, Sananda, Archangel Zadkiel, Mother Mary, and Saint Germain

Creative Change

"The country you know now as Canada is to serve as a Creative Land. It holds within it the space for thirteen Star seeds..."
- SANANDA

Welcome Beloved Children of the Golden Flame! I AM Sanat Kumara, and I shall be assisted by my Beloved Brother Sananda. I am here to bring forth this information that is known as the creative change for the continent of America, the country known as Canada. Dear ones, I am here for your assistance. I request permission to enter your energy fields.

Response: "Beloved Sanat Kumara, you have permission. Please come forth. I welcome you."

He and Sananda are now sitting down at a table and the map is unrolling.

Canada is to be known as the Land of Creation. Please pen this in!

Response: "Yes."

CANADA AND THE NEW HUMANITY

Dear ones, this beloved country has been brought forth to serve as a creative force, or to carry a space, as you have understood, for thirteen Star seeds.

You have understood what it takes to create a form; first, there must be a space that can contain it. These lands, once covered by ice, will now come forth in the glory and majesty of the Golden Age, flourishing in a series of islands, thirteen golden islands which hold a space, a creative space for each Star seed.

Beloved Sananda would like to speak.

Response: "Please come forward Beloved Sananda."

Dear ones, I AM your Brother Sananda. I ask permission to come forth into your energy fields.

Response: "Please come forward into our energy fields."

THE PERFECTION WITHIN

That area which is the island of the Tiny Christ I shall explain to you. It represents the ONE Perfect Cell within each human being. As you have understood the Cellular Awakening within mankind, it is that beginning source, the small source and Flame of Desire, Love, Wisdom, and Power which comes forth for the other cells to be duplicated by the rythmatic harmony of God! Dear ones, we call this "Tiny" as a great honor. What was once small in form now takes form into the consciousness of the planet Prahna!

Dear one, it is still my request that the Dove be present on all of these maps. Understand that it is the mighty grip of the talons of the eagle that is to be transformed into the peaceful heart of the Dove.

Response: "It is understood."

As the eagle has been the intake, the Dove shall represent the outtake, as one continuous breath.

What complements this great Law of Love that serves the universe? Strength, Dear ones. We call forth protection! And so what has been created here is a STRONG space, a space that protects the gentleness of that flowing and allowing creative force, Love.

Dear ones, this beloved country we shall now call the Land of Creativity. The country you know now as Canada is to serve as a creative land. It holds within it the space, again, for each of the thirteen tribes or Star seeds, the first Star seed to come in at the beginning of the 1,000 year period of Grace.

To the West, or what you know now as the west, soon to be what you refer to as East, is the Vortex of the Mystic Breeze. Beloved Portia will be serving here. She steps forth as the complement of Freedom, Justice, and Equality. And what would complement Freedom? JOY! The playful allowance of being! This comes forth to assist in the re-creation of this land. Do you have questions?

Question: "When it is appropriate, will you please check our boundaries and delineations? That is all. Please continue."

LAKE LOUISE

What is now known as Lake Louise has served these lands well, as a great focus for the Rays of the Great White Brotherhood. We would like you to footnote that this lake shall remain throughout all of the changes. It shall be renamed the Lake of the Inner Source, for the great Service that it has offered from its waters.

And from its waters, during this great Time of Change, many shall come and drink and become healed! For they contain within them a cleansing, clearing, and purifying vibration! It affects the rate of spin of the cells that have been duplicated out of alignment. Do you understand?

Question: "It is the increased rate of spin that allows the alignment to begin?"

Which allows it to align to what you know as the Flame of the Heart's Desire!

Land to the North of this Lake shall become just that, a Flame of Desire. This great Flame of Desire shall span up to the mountain's peak! It shall be clear and visible to many, carrying within it a pink and gold hue. For you well know that it is Desire that must step forth first within the heart of man, and then the Unfed Flame of Love, Wisdom, and Power may act accordingly, in alignment to the will.

Beloved, I turn the floor back to Sanat Kumara.

Response: "Thank you."

Greetings my Beloved children of the Golden Sun! I AM Sanat Kumara, and wish to continue discourse on what you know now as Canada.

GLOBAL WARMING

Held within the great grip of this Eagle Land, what she has been is one who has been filled with ice. That ice now thaws to reveal her doveness, her white morning breast! This land is now exposed as the Sun's great mothering. Nurturing Rays fall upon her. She steps forth to nurture and hold the space for the thirteen Star seeds. One may ask, is this all that a land should do, just to hold a space? What is that to hold a space? Do you not contain all elements of creation that have stepped forth to carry form? Do you not step forth with a momentum of energy and sustain and maintain, as we have discussed?

Dear ones, this is a great Service, to carry this heritage for the planet. For this is a Garden of Creation. This great land has been brought forth to hold this space, so that those who create may step forward as the creative, Golden Beings of Light that they truly are! Divine Land that you are, come forth in the star radiance of the Planet Prahna! You who have felt the inner core for so long, now yield yourself to the Rays of the Golden Sun!

Dear Land, I call to you. Step forth and breath the air and this Light and Love of God that Never Fails! I am here for your assistance Dear ones.

Question: "Can you see our map?"

I can see mine, Dear one, and impress to you what I see here.

A GOLDEN CITY DEDICATED TO THE VIOLET FLAME

Jeafray! We have spoken of the space of stillness, and that is what this area and Golden City will signify. Those who come will come to learn the space of stillness. And this is the celebration of the Violet Flame that comes forth!

The Violet Flame of Obedience. The Violet Flame of Grace. The Violet Flame of Forgiveness. The Violet Flame that transmutes all who come back to the Source, the ONE Perfected Cell I AM.

Toronto shall be known as the Obedient City. For those who stand within its radiance will understand the rhythm of stillness. There are those who experience stillness, and see and feel and hear no rhythm. But stillness is the timing of time. It is the space that exists between each beat. It is the space that exists between each season. It is the space that exists between each color. Stillness.

I step back, and allow Beloved Archangel Zadkiel to step forth!

I AM THE ARCHANGEL ZADKIEL, and I come forth to bless this city, the Obedient City of the Violet Flame! Mercy and Forgiveness touch all who come to this great land, and I shall serve the great Ray that sponsors the period of transition! I, as Zadkiel, AM a servant to this Flame, and those who come forth from here carry it in their hearts as lovers of truth!

He steps back, and Beloved Mary appears.

Dear one I AM Mary. May I be allowed to step forth into your energy field?

Response: "Please, Beloved Mary, come forth."

GREENLAND

We have mentioned Greenland and the island that shall be formed off of her coastline. While I hold my radiance into the Motherland, I have not forgotten what shall serve this great planet and her alignment, that steps forth to allow LOVE to stream into the hearts of man. The great strait which shall be formed allows access to a great Land of Abundance.

See, Dear ones, how each of these waters and islands all serve one another. Each has been allowed to step forth individualized! Each characteristic of this great land plays a part in what we call the symphony of transition. For humankind to recognize their divinity, they are to be shaken, in a sense, and given the gift of Love! For Love to stream forth into these hearts, hearts that have been fashioned, yes, by my hands, and the hands of the Mighty Creator I AM, they must be given the gifts of all of the universe.

CHOICES CREATE ABUNDANCE

This land shall represent the example. Each gift imaginable will be graced across this land, Canada. Each desire, each want, all that can be allowed to stream forth to the heart of man will come forth to this mighty continent, North America. And this island shall serve as a pivot point. What is known as Greenland shall thaw Dear ones and become a mighty, prosperous, abundant, true green land! What have we spoken of? But Abundance and the aboundness of choice. Prosperity again shall be the end result. This mighty land shall serve as having all the gifts of choice and all the gifts of creation! Dear ones, it shall serve as the playground for the great Manus to come forth. These children shall toddle upon her lands and waters and rejoice in the Grace of this planet. Do you have questions Dear ones?

Question: "Is Greenland still called Greenland?"

It shall be called the Aboundland. For it is bound in the abundance of the law. Dear one, if you do not have further questions, Beloved Hilarion would like to step forth.

Response: "I understand. Please step forth Hilarion. Thank you, Mary."

Greetings and Salutations, I AM Hilarion! I come forth from what you know clearly and truly to be the Green Ray! I shall represent here a focus for choice. I shall hold this for all who come to play with these great waters and lands. Creation shall step forth for all upon the planet and to those who travel to the Golden City in this land, I offer my Service! I offer myself in Service to you Dear ones, humankind, Cosmic Beings of this planet! I AM Hilarion, and come forth on the Green Ray! I offer Service to you, Dear ones, to the understanding that choice creates aboundness! Come and create with me!

Question: "I accept and thank you for your offer of Service. Is there anything else we need to know about this Golden City that you sponsor and minister?"

He is throwing both hands up in the air, and stars are falling all over this land.

As I throw these stars up into the sky, do you not see the many choices that they create? Light streams from each Ray and again another star is created. This is aboundness! Come to me and fill your purse Dear ones! There is plenty for all! There is always enough! This which is called the universal substance is indeed abundant and a dance of stars!

TAKE MY HAND

Welcome my Beloved chelas. I AM Saint Germain.

Response: "Welcome, Germain. Please come forward."

It is with great consideration that I step forward, for I AM indeed the CHOHAN OF THE SEVENTH RAY!

This is the end result of my project. I instruct you and ask you, Dear chelas and children, to observe these coastlines. Study them Dear ones, for we together shall create the accuracy.

Question: "Dear one, can you see our map?"

I am observing here with Beloved Sananda and Sanat Kumara.

I am running my finger down the map at this instant.

Question: "Would you care if I place my pencil upon the map?"

It is my request that you do so. And I shall bridge myself to you, my hand over your hand, my heart over your heart.

Question: "Is this an appropriate place to start?"

Start on the new East Coast. Start up in the Vortex of my Beloved Divine Complement, Portia!

Response: "I am in the center of the Vortex."

Now, feel my hand over your hand.

Proceed down the coastline. When you get down to the bottom, Dear one, you come to the island of the Morning Light. Place this name.

Question: "How are we doing?"

Adjust a little bit, Dear one. Proceed down. And off this mighty coast, a new land shall emerge.

Question: "Is this Island correct?"

There is an island that shall emerge approximately 800 kilometers from the most southern tip, which you know now as Alaska.

Dear one, it is only that I mention this, and we shall address it in further discourse.

Response: "Proceed."

[Editor's Note: This information progresses by an energetic transmission of Saint Germain's hand over Len's hand. Together, they refine the rough edges of the map of the Land of Creation, Canada.]

THE GOLDEN CITY OF BROTHERHOOD

The Bridge of Brotherhood, this serves as a connecting link between all the Brotherhoods. For in this Time of Transition that has existed upon your planet, people have engaged in much judgment of one another. Observe the beautiful BROTHERHOOD that exists, Dear one! Are there not Brotherhoods that exist between Mineral to Vegetable Kingdoms? Beautiful Brotherhoods that exist between animal to humankind? And within your own humankind, are there not beautiful Brotherhoods that exist between one race to the next? See the beauty in the vibrant Pink Race; the crystal, Blue Race; the golden Yellow Race; the shining White Race. Dear one, judge not one another, but recognize the beauty that each of you holds! Lady Master Venus has encouraged you to honor the Divine Form.

THE COAST MOUNTAINS

These mountains will serve to bridge the world of Divine Form. For it is, indeed, the Beloved Ashtar Command that has come forth to be of Service to the Spiritual Hierarchy of the Great White Brotherhood. This Service has come forth in great love! And while they are not Masters of this particular third density plane, they bring with them a Mastery that comes from their source. Dear Ones, we honor the work that they have offered to give. And this shall be the location that shall serve as one of their points of liftment. There will be, indeed, several star crafts, and in this mountain range shall be points of recovery. As the time comes near, these great beings will be brought back to this planet that they come from, Prahna. They shall then be ready to focus on Mastery. For again, they shall be offered the choice to Master third density on the new planet, Prahna!

Do you understand?

This shall occur in 500 to 700 years, within the period of Grace!

Question: "Is our mountain range correct in its direction?"

It curves out, into the sea. A series of islands erupt. There will be some volcanic disturbance up at the northern end of these islands; however, this shall dissipate within a 300 year period. Dear one, it is time for me to take my leave.

Response: "We shall pick up with you at this point next time."

At your request, I AM Saint Germain!

CHAPTER FORTY
with Sanat Kumara

Abundant Seas

*"There is plenty for all! There is always enough!
The Universal Substance is indeed abundant!"*
- HILARION

Welcome my Beloved Children of the Golden Flame. I AM Sanat Kumara. I step forth into your energetic bodies with your permission only.

Response: "Welcome Sanat Kumara, and please step forth."

I have come forth to complete this project, the Earth Change Map, which is to be called the Creative Land of North America!

Response: "Please continue."

We are in a room and he is standing over a map. To his left side is Sananda, holding in his hand a gold pen. He is sketching on this map, and showing boundaries, borderlines, and the new coastlines.

NEW SEALIFE

Dear one, it is important that you understand the oceans that surround these new land masses. Towards what we call Greenland, that ocean will be called the Abundant Sea. Within her waters will be many fishes of many kinds. You have thought that after the Times of Changes there would be no life upon your planet. The fish will remain in the Abundant Sea. This will be one of the first areas upon the planet that catches of many varieties occur. For you see Dear ones, there still will be those upon your planet that require the intake of such food into their systems. There are still other members of certain galaxies or solar systems that are coming to your planet to learn and to feel and to express themselves in being. Do you understand?

Response: "Yes, please continue."

NORTHWEST TERRITORIES

We have here the Diamond Seas. Sparkling within them is indeed the clear, crystal water that is to serve this period of time. The pristine waters will serve mankind and then reflect upon the purity and the innocence of the age that mankind enters into, for it is a period of Grace. Grace has been bestowed upon you. Grace is indeed a part of creation, for within Grace is contained the innocence and purity of faith and trust.

POLE SHIFT AND THE GULF OF ALASKA

To the West, which is now called the Pacific Ocean, which would touch the Bering Strait at one time, the ocean will be called the Sea of Ellipse. When you have the shift of the poles, North to South, these waters will indeed ellipse, and what once reflected the Sun will reflect the Moon.

CANADIAN WEST COAST

To the West Coast, the lands slip away and hold waters deep blue, for these are the waters of truth! They symbolize the deep reason of all things. These waters are navigable, and underneath them, many deep tunnels and caverns run into the interior of the land. Along this coastline will be the deep tunnels, where one may go to travel to the inland of Canada.

In future years, this will be developed as a form of transportation. Do you have questions?

Question: "Water transportation will be a Service in what is now the Pacific Ocean?"

It is the existing Pacific Ocean, what is known as the West Coast of Canada.

Question: "Which then will be called the East Coast? There will be tunnels to the central land mass of Canada?"

That shall go under what you call the first layer of the land itself.

Question: "Approximately how many kilometers deep is this?"

485.

Question: "Is this at a direct angle to the core of the planet? What is the angle of degree?"

Sixteen degrees.

Question: "The coastline that we now have is in Canada, which is part of British Columbia, and is towards Alaska and the Yukon Territory. Is there anything specific we need to know for this future eastern area?"

During the Times of Changes great torrential rains shall pelt this coastline. Dear ones, as the waters rise and the rains begin to fall, there shall be much monsoon activity in this area. However, as the skies begin to clear, it shall enjoy a prosperous, abundant, and somewhat tropical environment. Up toward what is now the North will be a cooler, temperate climate.

THE YUKON

Question: "This will be in the existing Yukon Territory?"

That is correct. However, much of the existing Yukon Territory will, in essence, float and break away.

Response: "Yes, I see that."

But the Alaskan state of the United States will, for the most part, remain intact, other than what is called the Northern Slope.

Question: "I understand. Will this also be a temperate climate?"

It shall share in the temperate winds from the Golden City of Balance and Equality, for the wind is brought to evenly distribute the force of water and fire.

Question: "There is a Golden City in the Alaskan area?"

There is one that sits by her border, which shall be governed by Beloved Portia: Eabra, the Mystic Breeze.

Question: "Is this actually in the Yukon Territory, close to the Alaskan Border?"

It is indeed, Dear one. And within this city, one shall travel to understand the balance and equality of the Elemental Forces.

Question: "Then it is safe to assume that each of the Golden Cities upon the planet is serving a purpose to expand experience and to perfect it?"

Dear one, theme and variation will be carried forth.

We stop and take a short break.

Response: "Dear Beloved ones, we ask for you to return to our energy force."

Welcome my Beloved children. I return. I AM Sanat Kumara.

Response: "Welcome Sanat Kumara. Come forward."

GLOBAL WARMING AND NEW TRANSPORTATION ROUTES

We have spoken of the caverns that exist for undersea travel within this country. You see, Dear ones, this will be a country where they will be developed as a form of public transportation. For the land that exists in the northern area of Canada is very unstable, indeed, particularly during the melting and thawing. This process will continue up to seventy-five years. This form of transportation shall be developed with the aid of our Beloved Brothers of the Celestial Realm, which you know as the Ashtar Command. This great Brotherhood has come forth to offer service technologies to aid mankind. For you see, Dear ones, for those who are not interested in attaining the Mastership, but those who are still interested in attaining the Ascension to Fourth Dimension, we are here to accommodate all who are on the path of guidance, and to encourage all to interact in a way which promotes harmony and peace on the planet.

CALGARY AND EDMONTON

Dear one, there will be several points of Ascension. There are two types of Ascension. There is the Ascension which is called the Rapture. Rapture occurs when a great many will be taken up. The city known as Calgary, shall be used as such a point for Rapture, Dear ones, and she shall be renamed as such, Rapture City of the Celestial Home.

Question: "The actual Ascension point is northwest of current locations of Calgary?"

There are seven points, to be exact. Each will follow out fourteen to twenty kilometers from the center of Calgary.

They will be known as the seven gems, each of them typified by the corresponding Ray. There shall be a guiding light; a great star shall align with this point, which is the point of Edmonton.

Question: "Edmonton will be the guiding light?"

It shall shine forth! And will contain a guiding beam to help those of the Celestial Realm to come forth. Do you understand?

Question: "One of the Angelic Realm?"

Dear one, this is the Celestial Brotherhood.

Question: "I understand. But the guiding beam must be an interface between the Celestial Brotherhood and humanity?"

Dear one, this is correct.

Contained within it is, indeed, a Vortex that has existed for many years. It was used during the times of Atlantis as you have known, and has been referred to in previous work as the Weather Crystal. This is another point of such.

Question: "This is an anchoring point?"

This is so, Dear one.

Question: "Do we need to know who is the guiding being for Edmonton? Or is this being yet to be named?"

Yet to be appointed, Dear one. It falls within the ranks of the work of Ashtar.

Question: "Oh, I understand. Is there any more information we need to have for the Province of Alberta?"

Only that it shall serve as a great anchoring point for those who leave through Rapture.

SASKATCHEWEN: NORTH AMERICA'S NEW BREAD BASKET

Question: "I understand. May we continue to Saskatchewen?"

Dear one, it is closely linked to the area known as the bread basket of North America. These lands shall remain much unscathed during the great Time of Change, for the hand of God has pressed upon them! You see, as you hold a ball within your grip, two hands are around it.

Response: "Yes, a large ball."

And the point where the most pressure is held, the palm. This is such a point, Dear one.

Question: "I see! So it is a point of continuous, contained pressure?"

This is correct, so less change occurs. On the other side of the globe, you will find the other point.

Response: "Oh! That would be in Mongolia."

This is correct, Dear one.

And so there are the points that are unchanged. However, because of the continuous pressure of the electromagnetic field, as you well understand, there are areas of depression that occur. You have the upliftment of the Cooperation

Mountains into the lower Americas, and then they continue on up.

CHAPTER FORTY
with Sanat Kumara

Sweet Smile

"When one enters into forgiveness they realize the perfection of their heart."
- SANAT KUMARA

We just left off with Saskatchewen. We talked about that being the bread basket. We have lost some of Manitoba. In short, Lake Winnipeg will drain below ground, and in essence there is a large aquifer that exists under most of Manitoba. We will be able at some point to drill into this area, because water will be a necessity at the Times of Changes and in the early part of the Golden Age. We were leaving off at a place where we could actually do the drilling, with existing latitudes and longitudes which will be measurable in that time, although the axis will be in a different place. There will be existing maps to guide this drilling, and hopefully, when we go back to channeling, Sanat Kumara will give those exact numbers.

Welcome Dear children. I AM Sanat Kumara, and as you have given permission for me to enter, I express further on the changes for the Co-creative Land.

Response: "Please do, Dear one. We have lost some of your discourse on Manitoba."

It is most important that I share with you the magnetic property of water.

Response: "Thank you."

THE AQUIFERS OF MANITOBA

Water contains within it a magnetic pole. Water is attracted to water; however, a body of water contains, even in its molecular structure, a negative and a positive charge. For the body of water is the microcosm of the macrocosom of the molecule of the water. So there are waters that are, indeed, created to spread, as you would say, or to flow to what they are attracted to. Now do you understand?

Response: "Yes."

And so Lake Winnipeg shall indeed be attracted to the waters of its like charge, a great aquifer that exists underneath this area. These waters have been held in great reserve.

Question: "May we have the existing latitude and longitude?"

89.6 to 121 degrees.

Response: "Thank you. This will greatly help the children of the future."

This is named the Reservoir of the Sweet Smile. Remember, Dear ones, these waters are indeed, sweet. They have been held back by the Beloved Mother Planet. All is contained on this planet for you to have and to hold your great vision of creation. Do you not see beyond the garden that this is a playground? This is a great place where you have come to create! A studio for the artist!

We move on the city you call Ottawa.

Question: "May I ask a question regarding the city of Winnipeg?"

Proceed, Dear one.

Question: "The city's new name?"

It is called Faith. For as these waters slip into what you call the void of Earth, it will take great Faith and reserve to understand.

Response: "I understand. Please proceed onto Ontario, if there is no further information."

OTTAWA, A CENTER FOR THE ARTS

In the next area is a great expression of creative art, art which is brought forth to express in the material, outer world. You have the expression of beauty in your inner world and inner life. You have the expression of beauty in your outer world and outer life. This area will provide a cultural experience and exchange for many, brought forth as the Song of God. For the Song of God is the great creative art. Beloved Paul the Venetian will be expressing the great beauty as blessed upon Venus. Ottawa shall be renamed the City of Beauty.

Question: "So all manner of art will be here?"

All expression of all manner of art.

Question: "Please continue Dear one. Is there more we need to know for the Province of Ontario?"

There is more that shall follow, Dear ones. This is what I have to offer you at this present moment.

Question: "Do you wish to conclude?"

It would be to our advantage, Dear one.

Response: "Thank you very much."

I AM the Light of God that Never Fails. I have come forth to bless mankind with this information!

CHAPTER FORTY-ONE
with Sanat Kumara and Sananda

Perfection of the Flame

"Held within the great grip of this eagle land, what she has been, is one who has been filled with ice. That ice now thaws to reveal her doveness, her white morning breast."
- SANAT KUMARA

Welcome my Beloved children. I AM Sanat Kumara. I step forth to give you the continued information for Earth Changes for the planet Prahna. You see, Dear children, the work that is being brought forth creates the space, for water to be filled into what is called a new skin. First, this skin must be fashioned. And what are we doing here but showing the fashion of what has been set forth, known as the design for the period of peace and harmony, which shall be sustained as the Law of Grace.

The Angels sing for this period of time, MAY PEACE AND PROSPERITY REIGN SUPREME ON THE PLANET PRAHNA! This is the song of the heavenly hosts that has been brought forth from the Spiritual Hierarchy of the Great White Brotherhood. This is now bridged from the Divine Brotherhood and the Celestial Brotherhood. Dear ones, Dear children of this golden time, we ask you to step forth on this mantle of consciousness in order for you to see, Dear ones, that this is indeed your time! To become as we are!

Response: "Please do come forth Dear ones! So that we may continue."

MAP OF CANADA

Let me describe this scene. Sanat Kumara is carrying a great staff. He has the map of Canada under his arm. Sananda is to his left. At his right is Archangel Zadkiel. The map is unrolling on the table.

Dear ones, I AM Sanat Kumara, with Sananda, my Beloved Brother and friend. We step forth together to sponsor this work, the Earth Change information for Canada, the great land of Co-creation! I am here for your questions, Dear ones. There is much that we brought forth in our earlier discourse. I would like to bring clarity and clarification to any questions you may have.

Response: "Yes, yesterday we lost track of the tape in the discussion of the Province of Manitoba."

The Great Land of Waters.

Response: "If you would recapitulate that discussion, I would be most appreciative."

WATER AND MAGNETIC ATTRACTION

We spoke of the magnetization of water, how water attracts itself. Dear ones, you know that water itself is a great magnet. You understand the Law of Attraction, and water in itself, because of its most sensitive nature, a feminine form as we would call it, is indeed the most attractive of all the elements. Do you understand?

Response: "Yes, I understand."

So you have this great body of water called Sweet Lake that exists in the land of lakes.

Question: "Lake Winnipeg?"

This particular body of water is and shall be attracted to a body of water much like itself. You have within a body of water a positive and a negative charge, which stands at the North and South magnetic poles. In a molecule of water, you have the same structure. Does not the microcosm reflect the macrocosm?

Response: "Yes, it does."

Coming to your planet, three shifts of the poles. Water will be drastically affected by these shifts. Tides will be drastically affected.

The pull of these waters shall be water to water. It is not a pull of water to land, as originally thought in gravitational pull, it is of water to water!

Response: "Like attracts like."

That is true Dear one. In your great Pacific Ocean there has been the attraction and pull of this ocean to the Great Salt Lake. For underneath the salt lake is another great ocean! And it has been this great ocean that has been pulling ocean to ocean, body of water to body of water, attracting poles to attracting poles.

Question: "Oh, is this great ocean the size of Washington, Oregon, and some of California?"

You are correct, Dear one. This has been the force that has affected much of the tidal pull. A great tidal pull has affected your Great Lakes in the North American Continent. And so, Dear ones, you have a great aquifer that exists in what you call the great land of lakes. This is a great underground lake, containing many caverns. At one time, this actual water existed upon the surface of your land. However, in the break up of what is called now Prahna, of the continuous disk, it was covered by not only the basalt lava flows, but the ridges of sand also.

Response: "Yes, I understand."

This great body of water, in the middle of the second polar shift, shall begin to spurt and whirl in a counter-clockwise direction. Like it is going down the drain.

For it shall be attracted to a body of water that is like itself. It is attracted to the great aquifer, and it shall drain to it.

Question: "I understand. Does the aquifer have a name?"

We would like to christen the waters, Sweet Smile of the Great Inner Source, or what we would call, Krehna.

Question: "It is done! I understand. Is there more we need to know regarding Manitoba?"

Only about the great drain regarding this wonderful Lake. You see, Dear one, it is this great aquifer that will sustain the nation in that area during the Time of Great Change. As we discussed yesterday, this is the area into which you could drill to find these waters.

Question: "Could you once again give us those directions?"

89.6 up to 116, and as far as 121.2.

Question: "Understood. We will make sure these are in the Atlas. The town of Winnipeg?"

The City of Great Faith!

Question: "Will that be affected by this draining?"

Dear ones, some of the water shall spill over, and there will be a cleansing effect in this city. They should understand also, if this is to happen, there should be some evacuation measures taken. Dear ones, this lake draining, and with the great counter-clockwise motion occurring, there will be some earth accompanying the drain.

Question: "I understand. Approximately when?"

We would ask that people consider the emotions happening in this Earth area.

Question: "It is understood. Does that conclude Manitoba?"

For the moment, Dear one. Remember, all that we give you at this moment is the energetic reasoning that we view with from where we stand. Do you understand?

Question: "I understand. From where on the Earth's field are we reading?"

We are reading approximately from the sixth layer of the field, which has been brought from the seventh.

Question: "So the precipitation to the fifth will probably not occur until at least another two years."

It takes approximately a one and a half to two year cycle to penetrate each of these layers.

Response: "I understand."

However, Dear one, you are well aware of time compaction, and as you come closer to the inner densities, there can be a quick response as they jump or attract to. Do you understand?

Response: "Yes. I have observed this in the Human Aura, that the energy moves much quicker at the closer fields to the body. Further away from the physical body, the energy moves at a different rate of speed."

You are most accurate.

ONTARIO: A NEW CULTURE OF BEAUTY

Question: "Shall we move onto the Province of Ontario?"

Here is contained the beautiful Golden City Uverno, assisted by Beloved Paul the Venetian. He has come to express the beauty of being, the beauty of creativity!

Creation is indeed a work. It is expressed as a work of art. Creativity upon your planet has been measured in terms of what you call the accomplishment. However, there is that creative work which is measured by the work of beauty that is brought forth. This shall be an area that will express in its entirety the work of beauty!

And so, from this Vortex Golden City area, Beauty and Cooperation shall be honored in Uverno, known as the Song of God. It shall be an area where one shall learn the timeliness and orderliness of the music of the beauty and cooperation of light. This is expressed through painted and artistic expression as the light of color and the light of shadows. One shall learn the work of black within your density! And the laws concerning its removal.

Here one will learn to balance the expression of thought and feeling to bring forth a work of art. This is a central part of human development in learning to become a Cosmic Being. But only here will one focus to learn to create, and to understand what it takes to sustain a creation. The Song of God has burst, not only in the wind, but has played with the heart of man! Thought and feeling, Dear ones, are the keys to bring into balance. Listen to this wonderful song!

Question: "Yes, may we diverge for one moment? Since we are speaking of creativity, is it, in essence, the focus of all who are incarnate on this planet to understand their own Oneness with creation and become responsible Co-creators?"

This is so Dear one, for there are those who create and cannot sustain the creation. And so where does it return to? To the Universal Source from where it came.

To sustain a creation shows that one has stepped forth to serve as a responsible party for creation. One then artfully draws from the Universal Source and is breathing that breath of Universal Life into his creation continuously!

HUDSON BAY AND JAMES BAY

Question: "This is understood. Thank you very much. Also in the Province of Ontario, we have a major city known as Ottawa."

This shall also be known as the City of Prashee.

Response: "Please continue with description of Prashee."

Prashee. The Harmony Of Sound. The Dance of Light. The Celebration of Form. All of these synthesize to the concept known as Prashee. The end result, cooperative beauty. This shall be expressed as a focus in Prashee. In terms of Earth Change events, before she takes on her Fourth Dimensional identity, there will occur a splitting within the town itself.

Response: "Please describe this splitting."

I'm going to describe what I'm seeing. And I'm going to ask for your confirmation. Is there a river running through the middle of this town?

Yes. There is a river that comes down through the newly formed Bay of Deliverance that will, in effect, run very much through the town of Ottawa and empties into the newly formed lake which is called Unity Lake.

Yes, the town is, in effect, split in half.

Dear one, you are accurate in your assumption, for this town Prashee, is accurately described as being split in half. One side shall express the feminine and one side shall express the masculine.

Question: "Shall one side express the sound and one side express the light?"

Dear one, it is in this city that sound and light will be expressed as masculine and feminine through form and structure.

Response: "I understand. Most magnificent!"

We are ready to proceed.

Question: "Now, Ontario borders the United States and the Great Lakes; the Great Lakes will become one lake, Unity Lake?"

This is so Dear one.

THE GREAT LAKES: UNITY LAKE

Question: "What are the effects of Unity Lake on this immediate area in Canada?"

Of course you will have the continual draining, and the draining of Lake Winnipeg into the great aquifer, the Waters of the Great Inner Source. Unity Lake is the reflection of the great Inner Source. This lake that you see upon the surface draws from these waters of the aquifer. While the aquifer is not as large around as you would perceive, it is of great depth. It's depth proceeds halfway into the mantle of the Earth. This is hard for your scientists to understand, but remember Dear ones, there was the time when the land was only a continuous disk. It floated on a continuous body of water. And inside your planet, the waters. It was primarily a planet of waters with a fiery core. Do you understand?

Question: "Do we still contain a fiery core?"

It still contains the fires of creation. Man has perceived that to get to the fiery core you must go through layer upon layer of earth substance. It is water, Dear ones! This was a continuous planet of water. This continuous round disk of earth, or land, Prahna floated upon it.

Question: "The plates of the existing geography still float upon water?"

They do Dear one. And now, for the continued discourse, I turn the floor over to my Beloved Brother and friend, Sananda.

Response: "Greetings, Sananda. Please do come forward."

BAFFIN ISLAND AND THE FINAL POLE SHIFT

Welcome children of the great golden fire! I AM Sananda and I am most pleased to be at your Service! I come forth to give the information for the remainder of Canada. That is to remain is the final resting point of what you will know as your polar end.

This is named Plateau of the Rising Sun! You are most accurate, Dear one! For this is the final resting place of the pole for the period of transition, entering the final era of Grace.

Question: "We have completed with Ontario?"

Yes, my Beloved.

Beloved Kuthumi will be in what is called the Mal-ton area, and, of course, his radiance will spread up into the Canadian lands. Beloved Sister Kuan Yin shall also be of Service to Beloved Brother Kuthumi, and her radiance shall be serving in Jeafray. Of course, Beloved Archangel Zadkiel will be serving there as well. However, the Archangel must be accompanied by a Cosmic Being.

Any land which comes forth to serve as a Co-creative land, for this time and period known as Grace, will come under the Jurisdiction of the Violet Ray.

Response: "I understand."

America *is* Service, Dear one. Do you understand?

Response: "Yes."

The United States serves as a great school of healing and teaching. Its Divine Complement is what steps forth as a self-realized country of creation, which Canada is to be. This is a land that has been brought forth for great Cosmic Beings to express their divinity!

May Peace Reign Over These Lands! And those who walk and tread upon these lands, and take of these waters, let them be creative beings! Made in the image and likeness of I AM THAT I AM!

Beloved Portia shall serve at one side and on the other shall be Beloved Kuan Yin. For this is indeed a feminine planet of creation and this country shall express this! Do you have questions?

Question: "Yes, do you wish to give a description of Quebec Province?"

THE CANADIAN EAST COAST

What you have depicted is accurate, Dear one. There will be some breaking up of the lands which is now known as the East Coast. There is some breaking up of the lands which are known to the North. There is the bridged land, Ascension Bridge, which leads one to the site of twilight, the never ending, continuous, Violet Ray, named Plateau of the Rising Sun. This is a place of celebration, for one to go to be within the Violet Flame at all times upon the planet Prahna. It is here that one shall go to express the joy and thanksgiving of Forgiveness! For when individuals enter into the Violet Flame, they realize the Perfect Cell within their hearts, step forth and duplicate it, and then extend the radiance of this Awakened Cell to their Brother and Sister. This is the transmuting and transforming Violet Ray which comes forth! It is of Service to the period of Grace.

> GRACE REIGN OVER THIS PLANET!
> GRACE REIGN OVER THIS COUNTRY!

This great country of creativity, in the image and likeness of I AM Canada!

Dear one, this area, plateau of twilight, Plateau of the Rising Sun, contains within it both those periods of time in the continuous form of the Light of God that Never Fails. For to forgive assures that light prevails. This is the transmuting and forgiving light. The Violet Sun! Do you have questions?

SAINT LAWRENCE RIVER AND SEAWAY

Question: "May we address the cities of Montreal and Quebec and this Province of Quebec? Quebec City and Montreal are both on the existing St. Lawrence River and seaway. Will there be changes on the seaway and will there be changes for each of these cities?"

Of course the Saint Lawrence River will extend in width, four times its size.

It will be called the Great River.

Question: "Will it flow into Unity Lake?"

You are correct, for at the Times of Changes, it will reverse its flow, and then flow into Unity Lake.

Question: "The cities of Montreal and Quebec, will each of these survive?"

Montreal shall be renamed the City of Many Hands. It will be noted for the many expressions of the Love of God!

MINI ICE AGE

Regarding the city of Quebec, Dear one, we are entering into the area of Beloved Kuthumi. Ice shall cover this area for approximately 250 years. However, as this land begins to thaw, and its purification is completed by the ice crystals, the crystalline form of water, it shall be noted for its pristine beauty from this crystalline form. However, a great purification comes forth over this land. It shall be known as the City of Stillness.

Question: "You are saying, that for a 250 year period, Quebec City will be silent?"

Is not silence golden?

All that we have given for this great land of creation, Canada, does it not contain all elements of all Twelve Jurisdictions? It is for the expression of perfection, Dear one, that we ask for this land to come forth!

PERFECTION OF THE SPIRITUAL FLAME

From South America, where the spark of desire is planted, and the flame is held and cradled, it is brought forth and mothered. Then the flame is brought forth and educated, and then it is perfected! Do you see this flame as it rises from South America to Central America, to the United States, and then to Canada? Canada is the crown, Dear ones.

It is the perfection of the Flame of Creation! It is as the expression of creation that we ask for this country to come forth!

TORONTO AND LAKE ONTARIO

Response: "When I look also on the map, I have not addressed one city."

Proceed.

Response: "This is the city of Toronto. From the looks of our existing map, it appears it will survive the draining of Lake Ontario."

It will survive Dear one; however, its inhabitants will abandon it.

They shall know when the time comes, Dear one. They shall know. Dear one, it is time for us to roll this map and to seal it within the heart of the Creator of Creators. Beloved Saint Germain has offered himself of Service to define all boundary lines for you.

Dear one, I roll this Map and seal it in the heart of the Holy of Holies!

Response: "Understood. Let this be so."

Welcome my Beloved chelas. I AM Saint Germain. I step forth to offer myself in Service to you.

Response: "Thank you Beloved one. Please come forward."

Thank you for your permission. I have made my appearance here to offer myself as the Hand of God, to pen these borders with the utmost accuracy so you will feel secure in what you present.

Response: "It is my request that you shall do this."

Hold out your right hand, Dear one.

Feel my hand over the top of yours!

Response: "Yes, I see it!"

Dear one, I ask for you to proceed with this work.

Question: "Shall I speak to you in my own inner consciousness?"

Dear one, I shall be with you and you shall hear my voice. I ask that you complete in no less than twenty minutes.

Question: "I understand, it is hard for you to withstand our density. Is there anything I can do to help?"

Proceed with this work!

Spiritual Lineage of the Violet Flame

The teachings of the Violet Flame, as taught in the work of I AM America, come through the Goddess of Compassion and Mercy Kuan Yin. She holds the feminine aspects of the flame, which are Compassion, Mercy, Forgiveness, and Peace. Her work with the Violet Flame is well documented in the history of Ascended Master teachings, and it is said that the altar of the etheric Temple of Mercy holds the flame in a Lotus Cup. She became Saint Germain's teacher of the Sacred Fire in the inner realms, and he carried the masculine aspect of the flame into human activity through Purification, Alchemy, and Transmutation. One of the best means to attract the beneficent activities of the Violet Flame is through the use of decrees and invocation. However, you can meditate on the flame, visualize the flame, and receive its transmuting energies like "the light of a thousand suns," radiant and vibrant as the first day that the Elohim Arcturus and Diana drew it forth from our solar Sun at the creation of the Earth. Whatever form, each time you use the Violet Flame these two Master Teachers hold you in the loving arms of its action and power.

The following is an invocation for the Violet Flame to be used at sunrise or sunset. It is utilized while experiencing the visible change of night to day, and day to night. In fact, if you observe the horizon at these times, you will witness light transitioning from pinks to blues, and then a subtle violet strip adorning the sky. We have used this invocation for years in varying scenes and circumstances, overlooking lakes, rivers, mountaintops, deserts, and prairies; in huddled traffic and busy streets; with groups of students or sitting with a friend, but more commonly alone in our home or office, with a glint of soft light streaming from a window. The result is always the same: a calm, centering force of stillness. We call it the Space.

Invocation of the Violet Flame for Sunrise and Sunset
I invoke the Violet Flame to come forth in the name of I AM THAT I AM,
To the Creative Force of all the realms of all the universes, the Alpha, the Omega, the Beginning, and the End,
To the Great Cosmic Beings and Torch Bearers of all the realms of all the universes,
And the Brotherhoods and Sisterhoods of Breath, Sound, and Light, who honor this Violet Flame that comes forth from the Ray of Divine Love—the Pink Ray, and the Ray of Divine Will—the Blue Ray of all Eternal Truths.

I invoke the Violet Flame to come forth in the name of I AM THAT I AM!
Mighty Violet Flame, stream forth from the Heart of the Central Logos, the Mighty Great Central Sun! Stream in, through, and around me.

(Then insert other prayers and/or decrees for the Violet Flame.)

Glossary

Aboundness: The Universal Substance is always present and provides a bounty of opportunity and multiple choices.

Abundance: The second of the Twelve Jurisdictions is the principle of overflowing fullness in all situations and circumstances based on the Law of Choice.

Age of Cooperation: The age humanity is currently being prepared to enter; it occurs simultaneously with the Time of Change.

Alchemy: The process of Transmutation.

Alignment: Convergence or adjustment.

Alpha and Omega: According to the Ascended Master system of Guardian Suns the ancient heart of our Great Central Sun was once known as Elohae-Eloha who gave birth to a dozen magnificent Suns. Alpha-Omega is the fourth of twelve Suns in this solar ancestry and this lineage includes yet again another twelve Suns. Helios-Vesta is the fourth in this family of Suns, and emits spiritual light and life to Earth and the other planets of our solar system. Alpha-Omega is the current Great Central Sun.

Andeo: The thirtieth Golden City located in Peru, Columbia, and Brazil, South America. Its qualities are consistency; its Ray Force is Pink and Gold; and its Master Teachers are the Goddesses Meru and Constance. The Golden City of Andeo is also known as the *City of the Feminine*.

Apex: The center, especially the top of a Golden City Vortex.

Apollo: Apollo and Diana serve as the second of the twelve Suns from the lineage of the Alpha-Omega Guardian Suns. The great Apollo is revered as the ancestral father to Saint Germain's heritage of spiritual knowledge and teaching. Additionally, Apollo is a sponsor for the Twelve Jurisdictions.

Archangels (the Seven): The seven principal angels of creation are: Michael, the Blue Ray; Jophiel, the Yellow Ray; Chamuel, the Pink Ray; Gabriel, the White Ray; Raphael, the Green Ray; Uriel, the Ruby Ray; and Zadkiel, the Violet Ray.

Ascended Masters: Once an ordinary human, an Ascended Master has undergone a spiritual transformation over many lifetimes. He or she has Mastered the lower planes—mental, emotional, and physical—to unite with his or her God-Self or I AM Presence. An Ascended Master is freed from the Wheel of Karma. He or she moves forward in spiritual evolution beyond this planet; however, an Ascended Master remains attentive to the spiritual well-being of humanity, inspiring and serving the Earth's spiritual growth and evolution.

Ascension: A process of Mastering thoughts, feelings, and actions that balance positive and negative karmas. It allows entry to a higher state of consciousness and frees a person from the need to reincarnate on the lower Earthly planes or lokas of experience. Ascension is the process of spiritual liberation, also known as moksha.

Ascension Valley: According to the I AM America Prophecies, Ascended Masters appear in physical form in the Golden City Vortices during and after the twenty-year period. At that time, Mass Ascensions occur in the Golden Cities, at the Star or center locations of these Vortices, and in select locations around the world, which are hosted by the complementary energies of Mother Earth. A model of this type of location is Ascension Valley located in the Shalahah Vortex.

Asonea: The Twelfth Golden City of the Americas is located in Cuba. Its qualities are alignment and regeneration; its Ray Force is Yellow; and its Master Teacher is Peter the Everlasting.

Aura: The subtle energy field of luminous light that surrounds the human body.

Awakening Prayer: The Ascended Masters Saint Germain and Kuthumi offer this prayer to assist humanity's individual and collective Spiritual and Cellular Awakening:

> Great Light of Divine Wisdom,
> Stream forth to my being,
> And through your right use
> Let me serve mankind and the planet.
> Love, from the Heart of God.
> Radiate my being with the presence of the Christ
> As I walk the path of truth.
> Great Source of Creation:
> Empower my being,
> My Brother,
> My Sister,
> And my planet with perfection
> As we collectively awaken as one cell.
> I call forth the Cellular Awakening.
> Let wisdom, love, and power stream forth to this cell,
> This cell that we all share.
> Great Spark of Creation awaken the Divine Plan of Perfection.
> So we may share the ONE perfected cell,
> I AM.

Balance: "Put into proper order."

Belt of Golden Light (or Golden Band of Light): This etheric Golden Belt of high-frequency energy has been in place since the early 1950s. It holds back catastrophic Earth Changes until humanity has a better chance to evolve. The belt also plays a significant role in mankind's spiritual growth.

Braham: The fourteenth Golden City of the Americas is located in Brazil, South America. Its quality is nurturing; its Ray Force is Pink; and its Master Teacher is the Goddess Braham. Braham literally means *the nurturer* and this Golden City is the second of the *Three Sisters* in South America.

Celestial Brotherhood: Similar to the Great White Brotherhood, the Celestial Brotherhood limits its members to the Angelic Kingdom. This includes the Angelic Hierarchy of: Seraphim, Cherubim, Glories, Thrones, Dominions, Virtues, Powers, Principalities, Archangels, and Angels.

Cellular Awakening: A spiritual initiation activated by Master Teachers Saint Germain and Kuthumi. Through this process the physical body is accelerated at the cellular level, preparing consciousness to recognize and receive instruction from the Fourth Dimension.

Chakra(s): Sanskrit for wheel. Seven spinning wheels of human-bioenergy centers stacked from the base of the spine to the top of the head.

Chamber of Symbols and Planetary Justice: An ethereal or Fourth Dimensional location where certain Ascended Masters meet. Chelas or initiates of Master Teachers are sometimes allowed entry into these concealed locations, however these incidents are rare. It is said the history of the Earth including her geography, flora and fauna, races of humanity, cultures, and societies are held in Akashic Records in the chamber, and many of their venerated symbols correspond to this information. Some esoteric students claim that the Chamber of Symbols physically exists as the Cave of Symbols, the assumed retreat of Saint Germain within the Earthly fissures of Table Mountain, near Jackson Hole, Wyoming.

Clarity: The third of the Twelve Jurisdictions lends lucidity to our perceptions through the Law of Non-Judgment.

Charity: The eighth of the Twelve Jurisdictions deems the generous actions of Charity as the everyday habit of living with love and equity.

Chela: Disciple

Chohan: Another word for Lord.

Christ, the: The highest energy or frequency attainable on Earth. The Christ is a step-down transformer of the I AM energies, which enlighten, heal, and transform all human conditions of degradation and death.

Circle of Fire: As human consciousness expands to the Fourth Dimension contact with the Elemental Kingdom is simultaneously achieved. This exchange influences Earth's collective consciousness and affects the Ring of Fire. Master Kuthumi teaches this spiritual process as the Circle of Fire to further conscious relations between humanity and Elemental Kingdoms. Mastery of this technique can lead to greater comprehension of planetary weather patterns.

Co-creation: Creating with the God-Source.

Collective Consciousness: The higher interactive structure of consciousness as *two or more*.

Consciousness: Awakening to one's own existence, sensations, and cognitions.

Cooperation: The seventh of the Twelve Jurisdictions advises joint actions, work, and assistance to faithfully adhere with fairness, honesty, and the acknowledgment of the Divine Presence.

Cradleland: South America, also known as the Motherland.

Creation-Creativity: The final spiritual precept of the Twelve Jurisdictions is best understood as the engendered Law of Divine Order.

Creativity: Creating with the God-Source.

Crotese: The sixteenth Golden City of the Americas is located in the Heartland countries of Costa Rica and Panama, Central America. This Golden City's qualities are *divinity* and the *Heart of Love*; its Ray Force is Pink; and the resident Master Teacher is Paul.

Cup: A symbol of neutrality and grace.

Desire: Of the source; the ninth of Twelve Jurisdictions and states the heart's desire is the source of creation.

Deva: Shining one or being of light.

Divine Spark: A Gnostic principle that God is contained in the human body. The Divine Spark is encouraged to grow and reunite with the I AM Presence.

Divinity: Derived from the Sanskrit word *Deva*, this notion is the transcendent power of light or God.

Dove: A symbol of peace and renewal.

Duality: An understanding that the world is divided into two perceptible categories.

Eabra: The seventh Golden City located in Canada in the Yukon and Northwest Territories. Its qualities are joy, balance, and equality; its Ray Force is Violet; and its Master Teacher is Portia.

Earth Changes: A prophesied Time of Change on the Earth, including geophysical, political, and social changes, alongside the opportunity for spiritual and personal transformation.

Earth Plane: The dual aspect of life on Earth.

Earth's Grids: Geometrical patterns that cover the Earth and follow symmetrical links to sacred geometry and crystalline shapes.

Earth's Energy Bodies: According to the I AM America teachings Earth's Energy Bodies correlate to five physical layer(s) of Earth's atmosphere. They are: First Light Body, Troposphere; Second Light Body, Stratosphere; Third Light Body, Mesosphere; Fourth Light Body, Thermosphere; Fifth Light Body, the Golden Grid.

Eighth Energy Body: A new light body that develops to assist the growth of Unity Consciousness.

Eighth Ray: The quality of this perceptible force of light and sound is evolved desire—the indelible connection to the source within. Its purpose fosters the awareness of the God within to individuals and groups, and ultimately assists the growth of humanity towards Unity Consciousness.

El Morya: Ascended Master of the Blue Ray, associated with the development of the will.

Elemental: A nature-being.

Elohim: Creative beings of love and light that helped manifest the Divine Idea of our solar system. Seven Elohim (the Seven Rays) exist here. They organize and draw forward Archangels, the Four Elements, Devas, Seraphim, Cherubim, Angels, Nature Guardians, and the Elementals. The Silent Watcher—the Great Mystery—gives them direction.

E-Motion: Conscious awareness of non-volitional feelings and emotional reactions that can cloud or assist Co-creative activity.

Emotional Body: A subtle body of light that exists alongside the physical body. It comprises desires, emotions, and feelings.

Energy Fields: Distinct and definable layers of energy that exist around all forms of physical life: mineral, plant, animal, and human.

Eyes to see; Ears to hear: *see Open Ears, Open Eyes*

Faith: The tenth of the Twelve Jurisdictions places confidence and trust in our innate creative birthright.

Feminine: Esoteric philosophy considers the Mother Creative principle as the highest expression of being. Femininity is akin to the Goddess; it comprises one half of God whose gender is neutral. Feminine energy represents love, beauty, seduction, sensitivity, and refinement—the characteristics of the Goddess Venus. On the dark side, it reflects vanity, superficiality, fickleness, and exhaustion. Femininity is the intuition, a nurturing force which, above all, produces the first creative spark in our Sun of Truth; the female essence serves as the inspiration and aspiration for life's goodness and purity—a devotion to truth.

Fifth Dimension: A spiritual dimension of cause, associated with thoughts, visions, and aspirations. This is the dimension of the Ascended Masters and the Archetypes of Evolution, the city of Shamballa, and the templates of all Golden Cities.

Fourfold Flame: The Threefold Flame exists in the heart and a fourth flame appears as the individual furthers their spiritual evolution. This is known as the Fourfold Flame. The four flames represent Love (pink); Wisdom (yellow); Power (blue); and Unity (white).

Four Robed Beings: The four white-robed Ascended Masters sponsor the I AM America teachings. They are: Sananda, Kuthumi, El Morya, and Saint Germain. Some I AM America teachings suggest these Master Teachers are overseen by the immortal avatar Babaji. These Master Teachers are often referred to as the *Four Pillars*.

Fourth Dimension: A dimension of vibration associated with telepathy, psychic ability, and the dream world. This is the dimension of the Elemental Kingdom and the development of the super senses.

Freedom Star: The Earth's future prophesied name.

Freedom Star Map: The I AM America Map of prophesied worldwide Earth Changes.

Galactic Web: A large, planet-encircling grid created by the consciousness of all things on Earth—humans, animals, plants, and minerals. Magnetic Vortices, namely the Golden Cities, appear at certain intersections.

Geometric Language: The symbols of sacred geometry.

Gobean: The first United States Golden City located in the states of Arizona and New Mexico. Its qualities are cooperation, harmony, and peace; its Ray Force is Blue; and its Master Teacher is El Morya.

Golden Age: A peaceful time on Earth prophesied to occur after the Time of Change. It is also prophesied that during this age human life spans are increased and sacred knowledge is revered. During this time the societies, cultures, and the governments of Earth reflect spiritual enlightenment through worldwide cooperation, compassion, charity, and love. Ascended Master teachings often refer to the Golden Age as the Golden-Crystal Age and the Age of Grace.

Golden City Grid: The matrix comprised of all Golden Cities covering the Earth.

Golden City Vortex: According to the prophecies, these large Vortex areas are havens of safety and spiritual growth during the Time of Change.

Golden Flame: An energy field of spiritual enlightenment. The teachings of the Golden Flame are said to originate from the Pleiades.

Golden Leafed Books: The Akashic Records from which the Twelve Jurisdictions were read and interpreted by the Ascended Masters. The Golden Leafed Books are said to materialize in the spiritually perfected retreats of the Ascended Masters.

Gold Ray: The Ray of Brotherhood, Cooperation, and Peace. The Gold Ray produces the qualities of perception, honesty, confidence, courage, and responsibility. It is also associated with leadership, independence, authority, ministration, and justice.

Grace: Neutrality, calmness, peacefulness.

Great White Brotherhood and Sisterhood (Lodge): This fraternity of ascended and unascended men and women is dedicated to the universal uplifting of humanity. Its main objective includes the preservation of the lost spirit, and the teachings of the ancient religions and philosophies of the world. Its Mission: to reawaken the dormant ethical and spiritual spark among the masses. In addition to fulfilling spiritual aims, the Great White Lodge has pledged to protect mankind against the systematic assaults—which inhibit self-knowledge and personal growth—on individual and group freedoms.

Guru: Another name for teacher.

Harmony: The first virtue of the Twelve Jurisdictions based on the principle of the Law of Agreement.

Heartland: Mexico and Central America.

Heart's Desire: This Ascended Master teaching recommends by identifying activities that yield personal joy and happiness, one may discover their Heart's Desire. The Heart's Desire is the wellspring of abundance, love, and creativity. Eastern philosophy often refers to this principle as the soul's specific duty or purpose in a lifetime—*Dharma*.

Hilarion: Ascended Master of the Green Ray and associated with the attainment of personal truth and the development of faith.

Hitaka: "So be it."

I AM: The presence of God.

I AM America Map: The Ascended Masters' Map of prophesied Earth Changes for the United States.

I AM Presence: The individualized presence of God.

Individualized: A state of wholeness and cannot be divided.

Illumination: The sixth of the Twelve Jurisdictions and gives light to our life without fear or judgment.

Jeafray: The eighth Golden City located in Quebec, Labrador, and Newfoundland, Canada. Its qualities are stillness and the celebration of the Violet Flame; its Ray Force is Violet; and its Master Teachers are Archangel Zadkiel and Amethyst.

Jehoa: The seventeenth Golden City of the Americas is prophesied to exist over new lands that rise in the Time of Change. The Golden City of Jehoa is located over the Lesser Antilles Islands of: Guadeloupe, Dominica, Martinique, Saint Lucia, Barbados, and Grenada. Its qualities are compassion, acts of love, and gratitude; its Ray Force is Violet; and its Master Teacher is Kuan Yin.

Jesus: *see Sananda*

Karma: Laws of Cause and Effect.

Klehma: The fifth United States Golden City located primarily in the states of Colorado and Kansas. Its qualities are continuity, balance, and harmony; its Ray Force is White; and its Master Teacher is Serapis Bey.

Kuan Yin: The Bodhisattva of Compassion and teacher of Saint Germain. She is associated with all the Rays and the principle of femininity.

GLOSSARY

Kuthumi: An Ascended Master of the Pink, Ruby, and Gold Rays. He is a gentle and patient teacher who works closely with the Nature Kingdoms.

Lady Master Venus: The celestial partner of Sanat Kumara, Lady Master Venus is the Goddess of Love, Beauty, and Sensuality. She is associated with all of the Rays with an emphasis on the White Ray.

Land of Creativity: Canada

Law of Agreement: The Master Teachers claim when two individuals move into ONE mind, truthful and honest motives are discovered by examining the personal actions of the parties involved. Successful agreements require commitment based on responsible choices and actions derived from the vital, creative source within.

Law of Allowing: The Law of Love, also known as the Law of Sustainability.

Law of Divine Order: Nothing happens by chance, and any event or creation is the result of choice. Simply stated, everything is in its proper place and order, according to the Divine Will.

Law of Grace: Transformation or regeneration through Forgiveness and Peace.

Law of Love: "If you live love, you will create love."

Law of Rhythm: Everything ebbs and flows; rises and falls. The swing of the pendulum is universal. The measure of the momentum to the right is equal to the swing of the left.

Laws of Attraction and Repulsion: Physically, like charges repel; unlike charges attract. Through the Spiritual Law of Allowing, like attracts like.

Lei-lines: Lines of energy that exist among geographical places, ancient monuments, megaliths, and strategic points. These energy lines contain electrical or magnetic points.

Light: "Love in action."

Love: "Light in action." The fourth of the Twelve Jurisdictions evolves our understanding of love as the Law of Allowing, Maintaining, and Sustainability.

Maltese Cross: The Maltese Cross, a symbol often used by Saint Germain, represents the Eight-Sided Cell of Perfection, and the human virtues of honesty, faith, contrition, humility, justice, mercy, sincerity, and the endurance of persecution.

Malton: The second United States Golden City located in the states of Illinois and Indiana. Its qualities are fruition and attainment; its Ray Force is Gold and Ruby; and its Master Teacher is Kuthumi.

Mantle of Consciousness: Ascending to or attaining a new level of conscious awareness that produces tremendous change.

Map of Exchanges: The Ascended Masters' Map of prophesied Earth Changes for Europe and Africa.

Marnero: The eleventh Golden City of the Americas is located in Mexico. Marnero means Virtue; its Ray Force is Green; and its Master Teacher is Mother Mary.

Masculine Energy: The Father creative principle. In esoteric literature, this is referred to as the Monad.

Master Teacher: A spiritual teacher from a specific lineage of teachers—gurus. The teacher transmits and emits the energy from that collective lineage.

Mastery: Possessing the consummate skill of command and self-realization over thought, feeling, and action.

Mental Body: A subtle light body of the Human Aura comprising thoughts.

Mind: The aspects of consciousness manifested as thought, perceptions, true memory, will, and imagination.

Motherland: A land of origin. The Ascended Masters refer to South America as the Motherland.

Mother Mary: Ascended Goddess of the Feminine who was originally of the angelic evolution. She is associated with the Green Ray of Healing, Truth, and Science, and the Pink Ray of Love.

Nada: The Ascended Goddess of Justice and Peace is associated with Mastery of speech (vibration), communication, interpretation, and the sacred Word. Nada is also known as a divine advocate of Universal Law and she is often symbolized by the scales of blind justice. She is associated with the Yellow Ray of Wisdom and the Ruby and Gold Rays of Ministration, Brotherhood, and Service.

New Age: Prophesied by Utopian Francis Bacon, the New Age would herald a United Brotherhood of the Earth. This Brotherhood/Sisterhood would be built as Solomon's Temple, and supported by the four pillars of history, science, philosophy, and religion. These four teachings would synergize the consciousness of humanity to Universal Fellowship and Peace.

ONE: Indivisible, whole, harmonious Unity.

Open Ears, Open Eyes: The ability to hear and see spiritual truths.

Pashacino: The sixth Golden City is located in Alberta and British Columbia, Canada. Its quality serves as a Bridge of Brotherhood for all people; its Ray Force is Green; and its Master Teacher is Soltec.

Paul the Devoted: A spiritual son of the three divine Suns: Krishna, Buddha, and Christ; this Ascended Master Paul represents the Eternal Heart of Love. He is associated with the White Flame of the Sun through the principles of purity, order, clarity, and mirroring the true nature of the soul. Paul is affiliated with the Pink and White Rays.

Paul the Venetian: An Ascended Master of the Pink, White, and Green Rays. Paul the Venetian identifies with the qualities of cooperation and beauty through art, architecture, music, and literature.

Perceive: To observe, feel, sense, and have awareness of.

Peter the Everlasting: This Ascended Master lived several controversial lifetimes on Earth; however, he found liberation through these everlasting spiritual precepts: balance, simplicity, and stability. He is also known as the consummate Master of Change and manages insecurity and unpredictability with the ever present wisdom of love and friendship. Master Peter is affiliated with the Yellow Ray.

Pole Shift: The Ascended Masters prophesy a pole shift and this geographical movement creates a change in Earth's energy fields. The final location of Earth's North Pole is Baffin Island, Canada.

Portia: The Goddess of Justice and Opportunity. She represents Divine Justice on Earth. Her action is balance, expressed as the scales. Harmony holds balance. Some say her electronic pattern, a mandala, is the Maltese Cross.

Prana or Prahna: Vital, life-sustaining energy. The Masters Teachers often refer to Earth as *Prahna*.

Prophecy: A spiritual teaching given simultaneously with a warning. It's designed to change, alter, lessen, or mitigate the prophesied warning. This caveat may be literal or metaphoric; the outcome of these events are contingent on the choices and the consciousness of those willing to apply the teachings.

Ray: A force containing a purpose, which divides its efforts into two measurable and perceptible powers, light and sound.

Rapture: An Ascension process assisted by the Celestial Brotherhood.

Ring of Fire: A geographical area, which encircles the basin of the Pacific Ocean, prone to volcanic eruptions and earthquakes.

Saint Germain: Ascended Master of the Seventh Ray, Saint Germain is known for his work with the Violet Flame of Mercy, Transmutation, Alchemy, and Forgiveness. He is the sponsor of the Americas and the I AM America material. Many other teachers and Masters affiliated with the Great White Brotherhood help his endeavors.

Sananda: The name used by Master Jesus in his ascended state of consciousness. Sananda means joy and bliss, and his teachings focus on revealing the savior and heavenly kingdom within.

Sanat Kumara: One of the original Lords of Venus who founded the Great White Brotherhood at Shamballa. He is also known as *Lord of the World*. The bible refers to him as *Ancient of Days*.

Seamless Garment: The Ascended Masters wear garments without seams. This clothing is not tailored by hand but perfected through the thought and manifestation process.

Serapis Bey: An Ascended Master from Venus who works on the White Ray. He is the great disciplinarian—essential for Ascension; and works closely with all unascended humanity who remain focused for its attainment.

Service: The fifth of Twelve Jurisdictions is a helpful act based upon the Law of Love.

Seventh Cycle: A crucial cycle Earth is now experiencing.

Seven Rays: The traditional Seven Rays of Light and Sound are: the Blue Ray of Truth; the Yellow Ray of Wisdom; the Pink Ray of Love; the White Ray of Purity; the Green Ray of Healing; the Gold and Ruby Ray of Ministration; and the Violet Ray of Transmutation.

Seventh Manu: Highly evolved lifestreams that embody on Earth between 1981 to 3650. Their goal is to anchor freedom and the qualities of the Seventh Ray to the conscious activity on this planet. They are prophesied as the generation of peace and grace for the Golden Age. South America is their forecasted home, though small groups will incarnate in other areas of the globe.

Shalahah: The fourth United States Golden City located primarily in the states of Montana and Idaho. Its qualities are abundance, prosperity, and healing; its Ray Force is Green; and its Master Teacher is Sananda.

Soltec: An Ascended Master of science and technology who is affiliated with the Green Ray.

Soul: The self-aware immortal essence unique to every living being

Spiritual Awakening: Conscious awareness of personal experiences and existence beyond the physical, material world. Consequently, an internalization of one's true nature and relationship to life is revealed, freeing one of the lesser self (ego) and engendering contact with the Higher (Christ) Self and the I AM.

Spiritual Hierarchy: A fellowship of Ascended Masters and their disciples. This group helps humanity through the mental plane with meditation, decrees, and prayer.

Sponsorship: To support and engender spiritual growth and evolution.

Stillness: The eleventh of the Twelve Jurisdictions produces the motionless quiet as the foundation of the Law of Alignment.

Star seed Consciousness: The Star seed is a family or soul group whose members have evolved to Fifth-Dimensional awareness. Star seeds can also contain members who have not yet evolved to this level and are still incarnating on Earth.

Tehekoa: The fifteenth Golden City of the Americas is located in Argentina, South America. Its quality is devotion; its Ray Force is Pink and Violet; and its Master Teacher is the Goddess Tehekoa, the Third Sister of South America.

Terra: Earth

Third Eye: The inner eye, referring to the Ajna (Brow) Chakra.

Thought, Feeling, and Action: In Ascended Master teachings and tradition, thought, feeling, and action are the cornerstones of the creation process. Thought represents the mental (causal) body and the Yellow Ray. Feeling represents the emotional (astral) body and the Pink Ray. Action represents the physical body and the Blue Ray.

Threefold Flame: *see Unfed Flame*

Three Sisters: Four Goddesses who represent the three feminine aspects of consistency, devotion, and nurturing to oversee and protect South America during the Time of Change and guide her entry into the New Times.

Time Compaction: An anomaly produced as we enter into the prophesied Time of Change. Our perception of time compresses; time seems to speed by. The unfolding of events accelerates, and situations are jammed into a short period of time. This experience of time will become more prevalent as we get closer to the period of cataclysmic Earth Changes.

Time of Change: The period of time currently underway. Tremendous changes in our society, cultures, and politics in tandem with individual and collective spiritual awakenings and transformations will abound. These events occur simultaneously with the possibilities of massive global warming, climactic changes, and seismic and volcanic activity—Earth Changes. The Time of Change guides the Earth to a New Time, the Golden Age.

Time of Transition: A twelve-year period when humanity experienced tremendous spiritual and intellectual growth, ushering in personal and global changes. In the year 2000 a new era, called the *Time of Testing*, got underway. It's a seven-year span of time when economies and societies encountered instability and insecurity. These years are also defined by the spiritual growth of humanity; Brotherly love and compassion play a key role in the development of the Earth's civilizations as mankind moves toward the *Age of Cooperation*.

Transmutation: Alchemy and the transformation of a lower energy into a higher energy, nature, or form.

Twelve Jurisdictions: Twelve laws (virtues) for the New Times that guide consciousness to Co-create the Golden Age. They are Harmony, Abundance, Clarity, Love, Service, Illumination, Cooperation, Charity, Desire, Faith, Stillness, Creation/Creativity.

Unfed Flame: The Threefold Flame of divinity that exists in the heart and becomes larger as it evolves. The three flames represent Love (pink); Wisdom (yellow); and Power (blue).

Universal Laws: Laws that apply to the entire universe; considered a fundamental basis of nature and reality.

Uverno, Golden City of: The Canadian Golden City of the Pink Ray. Also known as the Song of God, the Golden City Vortex is located primarily in Ontario, and Manitoba, Canada.

Violet Flame: The Violet Flame is the practice of balancing karmas of the past through Transmutation, Forgiveness, and Mercy. The result is an opening of the Spiritual Heart and the development of bhakti—unconditional love and compassion. It came into existence when the Lords of Venus first transmitted the Violet Flame, also knows as Violet Fire, at the end of Lemuria to clear the Earth's etheric and psychic realms, and the lower physical atmosphere of negative forces and energies. This paved the way for the Atlanteans, who used it during religious ceremonies and as a visible marker of temples. The Violet Flame also induces Alchemy. Violet light emits the shortest wavelength and the highest frequency in the spectrum, so it induces a point of transition to the next octave of light.

Violet Ray: The Seventh Ray is primarily associated with Freedom and Ordered Service alongside Transmutation, Alchemy, Mercy, Compassion, and Forgiveness. It is served by the Archangel Zadkiel, the Elohim Arcturus, the Ascended Master Saint Germain and Goddess Portia.

Vortex: A Vortex is a polarized motion body that creates its own magnetic field, aligning molecular structures with phenomenal accuracy. Vortices are often formed where lei-lines (energy meridians of the Earth) cross. They are often called power spots as the natural electromagnetic field of the Earth is immensely strong in this type of location.

Wahanee: The third United States Golden City located primarily in the states of South Carolina and Georgia. Its qualities are justice, liberty, and freedom; its Ray Force is Violet; and its Master Teacher is Saint Germain.

Will: Choice.

Yuthor: The tenth Golden City is located in Greenland. Its quality is abundance of choice; its Ray Force is Green; and its Master Teacher is Hilarion.

Index

A

A-bound-ness 201, 312
  definition 353
abundance. *See also* Twelve Jurisdictions
  and agreement 199
  and prosperity 201
  and spiritual teachings regarding choice 197
  and the Law of Harmony 199
  and vibration 198
  definition 353
"Abundance is a natural flow of choice." 199
Abundant Sea: Greenland 320
Africa 129, 146, 188
Age of Cooperation 59
Agreement 98, 187, 195, 199, 202, 205, 236, 245, 251, 271. *See also* abundance
  and divinity 241. *See also cooperation*
Agricultural Areas
  United States and Canada 77
Akashic book 196, 206, 214, 239, 253, 260, 274, 277, 291, 298. *See also* Golden Leafed Books
Alaska 69, 81, 322
  new island forms 315
Alberta, Canada 326
Albuquerque, NM 55, 77, 87
Alchemy
  definition 353
alignment
  definition 353
Alpha and Omega
  140, 141, 160, 161, 353
Amazon Valley 142
Amethyst City: ethereal city over Cuba 165
ancient geography and poles 266

Andeo
  Golden City of 171, 172, 353
Andes Mountains. *See also* Nativity Mountains
  relationship to each of the seven original civilizations 139
angels 290, 294, 296
  of sound 291
  Seven Archangels 353
angels of creation 263
apex
  definition 353
Apollo 215, 220, 281, 285, 287, 289, 297, 298, 353
aquifers 329, 336, 337, 343. *See also* Lake Winnipeg; *See also* Reservoir of the Sweet Smile
Archais
  the Angel 144
Archangel
  accompanied by Cosmic Being 344
  Chamuel 189, 274, 287
  Michael 189, 196, 221, 233, 239, 251, 260, 274, 277, 287
    Blue-White Flame 94
    sacrifice 215
  Raphael 287, 290
  Zadkiel 287, 311, 334, 344
Argentina. *See also* Patagonia
Arizona 53. *See also* Bay of Harmony
Ascended Beings 39
Ascended Master
  definition 353
Ascended Masters. *See also* communicating with the Ascended Masters
  and sensing ability 209
  and their Service 230
  communicate through like vibration 105
  purpose in the Golden Cities 45
  right hand over heart 297
  Who are they? 40
  work with Messengers 99

Ascension 47, 59, 60, 346
   and the sixth race 166
   mass 59
   process and Motherland 124
   two types 325
Ascension Valley 47, 59, 354
   location 47
Ashtar Command 317, 324
Asonea
   Golden City of 145, 354
Asteroid
   three month warning 68
Atlantis 108, 167, 176, 326
Awakening Prayer 213, 354

B

Baffin Island. See also Plateau of the Rising Sun
Bahamas. See also Star Island
Baja Peninsula: Mexico 106. See also Diamond Islands
balance 355
   spiritual teachings on 190
bartering 142. See also monetary system
Bay of
   Cooperation
      New Orleans, LA 76
   Deliverance
      James Bay, Canada 342
   Divinity
      Baja, Mexico 106
   Harmony
      Southwestern and Western United States 55
   Hope
      Argentina, South America 176
   Reconciliation
      New York City, NY 78, 86, 88
   the Golden Sun
      Gulf of Mexico 160, 161

Beauty 239, 241, 245, 332, 340
"Beauty sees the exquisite boundaries of each individual." 239, 245, 277, 295
Bismarck, ND 77, 83
black hole 191
Boise Basin, Idaho 73
Braham
   Golden City of 172, 355
Brasilia, Brazil 175
Brazil 121, 142, 171
bread basket 327, 329. See also Agricultural Areas
breath 281
Bridge of Brotherhood: Alberta, Canada 316
British Columbia, Canada 63, 322

C

Calgary, Alberta 325. See also Bridge of Brotherhood
   and seven Ascension points 325
California 48, 54, 336. See also Bay of Harmony; See also Pathway Islands; See also Gibraltar Island
Canada 55, 77, 82, 102, 305, 307, 309, 312, 316, 321, 324, 334, 343, 345
   opens the earth's crown chakra in the New Times 348
   prophecies of monsoons and rain 322
Cascade Range. See also Islands of Fortune; See also Bay of Prosperity
   becomes islands 48, 63
cataclysms. See also Time of Transition
   none during the Time of Transition 113
Catalina Island, CA 83
Cayce, Edgar 77
Celebration Island. See also Harvest Bay
   New Orleans, LA 85
Celestial Brotherhood
   angelic realm 326, 355

INDEX

Celestial Realm 324
Cellular Awakening 229, 306, 355
Center of Exchange: South America 142
Central America 105, 122, 129, 348. *See also* Cradleland
chakra 118, 192, 355
Chamber of Planetary Justice 196
Chamber of Symbols 271, 286, 295, 355
Chamuel. *See* Archangel: Chamuel
charity. *See also* Twelve Jurisdictions
  and giving 254
  and love 255
  and the joy of giving what we are 256
Charleston, NC 68
chela
  definition 355
Chicago, IL 55, 67, 73
chohan
  definition 355
Chohan of the Americas
  Saint Germain 119
choice
  spiritual teachings of 169
Christ Consciousness 40
Christ Self 94
Christ, the
  definition 356
Circle of Fire 133, 356
City of
  Beauty
    Ottawa, ON 332
  Prashee
    Ottawa, ON 341
civilization
  seven original 140
clarity. *See* Twelve Jurisdictions
  and judging or discerning 207
  and the open flow of energy 212
climate and wind patterns 78
Coast Mountains. *See also* British Columbia, Canada

co-creation
  definition 356
co-dependency 100
Coeur d'Alene, ID 47, 76, 77. *See also* Transportation Center
collective forgetting 241, 262
Colorado 53
Columbia River 44, 63. *See also* Bay of Prosperity
Columbia, South America 44, 63, 322
commitment 98
communicating with the Ascended Masters 39
Communication Center 84
completing what you start 179
Connecticut. *See also* Bay of Reconciliation
consciousness 40, 41, 192
  collective 116, 138, 205
Continental Divide 55, 67, 76, 84
cooperation. *See also* Twelve Jurisdictions
  and agreement 245
  and beauty 241
  and divinity 241
  and honor 241
  carry (hold) divinity 249
  feminine 240
  for a 1,000 year period 246
  masculine 247
  releases struggle 247
  "two who work..." 240
Cooperation Mountains 108, 120, 327
Cortez 155
Cradleland 356
Cradleland: South America 188
  underground bases 143
Crater Lake, OR 49
creation. *See also* Twelve Jurisdictions
  and the Four-fold Flame 298
  and the pure heart 291
  and the Twelve Rays 292
  as love, desire, sweetness of being 292

"Creation, see it pulse with the sweetness of life.
The joy of giving the Law of Love!" 293
creative wave 181, 184, 193, 210, 219, 226, 300
creativity
 and Oneness 301
 as active energy 299
 expression of creation 300
Crotese
 Golden City of 145, 356
crystal 61, 79, 138, 192, 316, 320, 326
Cuba 153, 155, 164
cup
 Chalice of Life 118
 definition 356

D

Dakotas, USA 55, 66, 77
Dallas, TX 88
Denver, CO 55, 56, 67, 71, 72, 77, 82, 84. *See also* Klehma: Golden City of
desire. *See also* Twelve Jurisdictions
 as genetic code 261
 as source 264
 definition 356
 Flame of 308
 illumined 288
 of the heart and creativity 263
 Spark of Desire 261
 the Eighth Ray 288. *See also* Ray(s): Eighth
Deva
 definition 356
Diamond Islands: Baja Peninsula 80, 106
Diamond Seas: Northwest Territories, Canada 320
dimensions
 space between 272
divine spark 241, 244
 definition 356

DNA coding 229
doubt 242
 cellular 267
dove 171, 307
 definition 357
duality 138
 definition 357

E

Eabra. *See also* Portia
 Golden City of 357
earth. *See also* ancient geography and poles; *See also* night and day: origins
 ancient geology 343
 and energy movement 266
 birth into the New Times 104
 element 111
 energy layers and their relationship to the human aura 134
 evolution 116
 shift and fourth dimensional awareness 188
 the first race 120
Earth Changes
 definition 357
Earth Plane
 definition 357
earthquake 51, 67, 144, 278
earth's core 343
earth's layers 134
 and energy fields 338
 and light bodies
  definition 357
economy 72
Edmonton, Alberta 325
ego 135, 234
Egypt 76
eighth energy body
 definition 357
Eighth Ray 288, 292
 definition 357

INDEX

Elemental
  definition 357
Elemental Life 128, 132, 133
El Morya 39, 134, 159, 188, 213, 285, 287, 295, 357. *See also* Gobean: Golden City of
Elohim
  definition 357
Emerald Islands: Mt. Shasta, CA 49, 75, 82
Emergence-Ressurrection 118
E-motion 220, 300, 301
  definition 357
emotional body 118
  definition 357
energy body
  human
    relationship to light 267
energy fields
  definition 358
energy techniques
  for manifestation 91
England 163, 189
enlightenment 235. *See also* illumination
equator 64, 81, 189
Europe 73, 146, 163, 188
Everno Island: Cuba
  Cuba 155

F

faith. *See also* Twelve Jurisdictions
  and stillness 274
  and the Rays 275
  light and strength 275
"Faith that brought me here and kept me here!" 276
fear 40, 52, 95, 106, 129, 149, 171, 201, 233, 235
feminine 216, 241, 244, 335, 351
  definition 358
Fifth Dimension 146
  definition 358

fire
  element 111
fish 320
Flame of Divinity 242
Florida 57, 61, 78, 86, 153, 163, 167, 176
Four-fold Flame 289, 298
  definition 358
four robed beings 38. *See also* Ascended Masters
Fourth Dimension 106, 110, 111, 117, 118, 124, 127, 133, 138
  awareness 188
  definition 358
free will 98, 179, 242, 275
fresh water sea 121. *See also* Lake of Mirrors

G

Galactic Web 146
  definition 358
geometric language 272, 277
  definition 358
Gibraltar Island
  Sierra Madre Mountains, CA 83
glacier movement 122
glaciers 123, 161, 162
Gobean
  Golden City of 54, 55
gold
  liquefied 161
gold and silver 68, 72
Gold Capstone
  off the Eastern coast of Florida 57
Golden Age 38, 48, 56, 61, 164, 172, 306, 329
  definition 359
Golden Band
  of protection 81, 355

Golden Cities 48, 51, 68, 71, 153, 324
  Maltese Cross and sacred geometry
    54, 65, 68, 69, 80, 85, 172
  nerve endings 49
  pyramid structure 49, 57, 60, 82, 166
Golden City 54, 60, 313, 323, 340
Golden City Grid
  definition 359
Golden Crystal Age 48, 80
Golden Flame 247, 251, 296, 305, 319
  definition 359
Golden Leafed Books 196, 260. *See also* Akashic book
  definition 359
Grace
  1,000 year period of 288, 307
  definition 359
Greater and Lesser Antilles. *See also* Silver Crystal Mountains
Great Lakes 54, 75, 78, 86, 336, 342
  drain 55
  formation of Unity Lake
    54, 65, 75, 78, 86, 336, 342
Great River
  St. Lawrence River, Canada 347
Great White Brotherhood 37, 191, 251, 285, 308, 317, 333
Greenland 311, 320
  Land of Abundance 312
Gulf of Alaska. *See also* Sea of Ellipse: Gulf of Alaska
Gulf of Mexico
    44, 66, 113, 160, 161. *See also* Bay of the Golden Sun
guru
  definition 359

H

harmony
  and alignment 190
  and ascended beings 191
  "Balance is the continuous cycle of harmony." 187, 195, 205, 213
Harvest Bay
  Texas and Louisiana, USA 83
Hawaii 69
  return to ancient culture 69, 81
Hawaiian Islands 80
heart
  chakra 133
  never forgets 242
Heartland: Mexico and Central America
    130, 154, 159, 164, 360
Heart's Desire
  definition 360
Hilarion 313, 360
Hitaka
  definition 360
Holy of Holies 215
honor 239, 245
Hudson Bay. *See also* Bay of Deliverance
human aura 339
human development
  through the arts 340

I

I AM
  definition 360
I AM America Map 360
I AM Presence 91, 94, 118, 129, 208, 214, 217, 262, 285
  definition 360
I AM THAT I AM
  and stillness 281
  "I AM the resurrection and the light." 165

ice 77, 81, 86, 122, 123, 162, 163, 167, 306, 309, 333, 347. *See also* Global Warming
  glacial ice caps, melting and formation 164
  melting, rising oceans 64
ice sheets 163
Idaho 47, 49, 82
ideas 236
Illinois 67
illumination. *See also* Twelve Jurisdictions
  and enlightenment 234
  and knowing 234
  and the illumined mind 236
  as choice 235
  "Illumination is the use of your mind without fear and judgement." 233
Island of Vision: New York, USA 88
Islands of Fortune: Pacific Northwest, USA 64. *See also*

J

Jacob's ladder 208
Jeafray
  Golden City of 310, 344
Jehoa
  Golden City of 145, 360
Jesus
  Sananda 119
judgment 242
Juneau, AK 81

K

Kansas 56
karma 40, 353
  definition 360
Klehma
  Golden City of 72, 360
Kuan Yin 115, 120, 170, 174, 188, 214, 285, 287, 290, 295, 344, 345
  Saint Germain's guru of the Violet Flame 351

Kuthumi 39, 71, 91, 92, 114, 115, 119, 131, 134, 146, 167, 188, 213, 214, 285, 287, 295, 344, 347, 361
  influence in Canada 344

L

Lady Master Venus 239, 245, 295, 361
La Grande, OR 48, 79
Lake
  Louise 308
  Michigan 75, 78
  of Mirrors 121, 127, 129, 140, 165
  of Mirrors: Caribbean Sea 49
  of the Inner Source 308
  of the Inner Source: Lake Louise 308
  Ontario 349
  Winnipeg 329, 335, 343
Law of
  Agreement 187, 195, 205, 213, 223, 233, 239, 245, 277, 285, 295
    definition 361
  Allowing, Maintaining, and Sustainability
    definition 361
  Attraction and Repulsion
    definition 361
  Commitment 98
  Divine Beauty 241
  Divine Order 285
    definition 361
  Grace 214
    definition 361
  Love 94, 218, 235, 276, 288, 289, 291, 293, 307
    definition 361
  Mercy and Forgiveness 94, 97. *See also Violet Flame*
  Non-Judgment 355
  Rhythm
    definition 361

leaving the conventional way of life 98
lei-lines
    definition 361
"Let there be light." 291
Lewiston, ID 73, 77
light
    definition 361
Livingston, MT 83
Lori Toye's dream 37
Los Angeles, CA 83
Louisiana 60
love. *See also* Twelve Jurisdictions
    and choice 217
    as allowing 216
    as a principle of creation 215
    as maintenance, the maternal energy 216
    as sustaining, the paternal energy 216
    definition 361
    order and the eternal flow 214
    sustains life 216
"Love, in Service, breathes the breath for all." 223
Love, Wisdom, and Power 157

M

Maine 57, 77, 78, 86
Maltese Cross 65
    definition 361
Malton
    Golden City of 362
Manitoba 329, 334, 337
Mantle of Consciousness
    definition 362
Map of Exchanges 362
Map of Exchanges: Europe and Africa 146
Marnero
    Golden City of 145, 172, 362. *See also Mother Mary*
Mars 95
masculine 95, 216, 247
    energy
        definition 362

mastery
    definition 362
Maui 80
meditation 92, 135
mental body 91, 118, 134, 136, 242, 249
    definition 362
Mesa, AZ 53, 55, 78, 82. *See also*
meteor 67
meteorites 51
Mexico 44, 55, 56, 66, 80, 106, 107, 109, 112, 113, 145, 153, 160, 161
Michael. *See* Archangel: Michael
mind
    and choice 234
    definition 362
mineral deposits 81, 192
minerals
    new 143
Mississippi 66
    widens 44, 54, 55, 56, 66
Mississippi Valley
    karmic affiliation to Ancient Egypt 76
Missoula, MT 76
Missouri 44, 83
Missouri River 83
moksha 354
monetary system 68, 72
Mongolia
    a safe land 327
monsoon winds 112
Montana 55, 83
Montreal, Quebec 347
Mother Earth
    assists the cleansing of the lower energy bodies of humanity 93
Motherland: South America 129, 146, 148, 150, 151, 162, 164, 175, 311, 362
Mother Mary
    115, 285, 290, 295, 311, 362
    immaculate conception 165

INDEX

Mount Shasta 49, 65
Mu 107
music
 and color 268

N

Nada 189, 362
New Age
 definition 362
New Consciousness 41
new flora and fauna 161
New Mexico 55
New York 43, 61, 78, 86
night and day
 origins 267
Norfolk, VA 86
North America 122, 124, 312, 319, 327
North Dakota 77
Northern Slope: Alaska, USA 323
North Pole 69, 266
 New Vortices point to magnetic North 64, 69, 266

O

ocean current
 changes 162
Okonagan Valley: British Columbia, Canada 63
Olympic Peninsula: Washington State 63
OM Vibration
 sung by Solar Angels 264
ONE 101, 169, 190, 213, 246, 291, 310
 definition 363
Oneness
 new form of communication 84, 136, 174, 299, 300, 301, 302, 340
Open Ears, Open Eyes
 definition 363
Oregon 48, 51, 79, 336
Oriental Cultures
 Alaska and Hawaii 81
Ottawa, Ontario 331, 332, 342

P

Pacific Northwest 53, 77
Pashacino
 Golden City of 363
passion 219
Pathway Islands
 California 82
Paul 115, 120, 123, 170, 189, 332, 339, 363
Paul, the Venetian 332, 363
Pennsylvania 86
perceive
 definition 363
Peru 139, 171
Peter the Everlasting 154, 363
Philadelphia, PA 61, 86
Phoenix, AZ 88
Pillar Peaks: Silver Crystal Mountains 157
Plateau of the Rising Sun: Baffin Island, Canada 344
pole shift 87, 321, 363
political centers 62
Portia 285, 287, 295, 307, 315, 323, 345
Prahna 292, 310
 another name for planet earth 287
 definition 363
Prophecy 106, 175
 definition 363
Pullman, WA
 WA 63

Q

Quantain
 solar system of 124
Quebec 345, 347
 prophecy of ice 347

R

Raphael. *See* Archangel: Raphael
rapture 325, 326, 363. *See also* Ascension: two types
Ray(s)
  Black 268
  Blue 152, 214, 261
  definition 363
  Eighth 247
  Eight Rays of Precipitation 298
  Gold 291
    definition 359
  Green 291
  Pink 123, 152, 214, 261
  Seven
    definition 364
  Violet
    definition 366
Reconciliation Bay: New Jersey and New York, USA 61
records
  of past civilizations 61
red skies 138
Reservoir of the Sweet Smile 331
resurrection 85, 107, 117, 165
Resurrection Body 118
Resurrection Island
  Baja, Mexico 107
Rhythm, Law of
  definition 361
Ring Map 146
Ring of Fire 167
  definition 364
  esoteric meaning and purpose 133
Rio de Janeiro, Brazil 144
River of
  Cooperation: Mississippi 55, 85
  Opportunity: Missouri 83, 85
Rocky Mountains 55. *See also* Cooperation Mountains

S

safe lands. *See also* Mongolia
  Montana and the Dakotas 44, 55, 83
Saint Germain 39, 364. *See also* Wahanee: Golden City of
  a bridge to freedom 286
  and the flame of freedom 119
  and the sacred fire 351
  Chohan of the Seventh Ray 214, 259
  spiritual heritage 353
  sponsor of the Americas 188
Saint Lawrence River 347
Salamander of Fire 109
Salt Lake: Utah, USA 75, 336
Sananda 39, 364
  and the blue-bird 302
  and the seed of Christ Consciousness 306
Sanat Kumara 187, 223, 228, 233, 245, 248, 251, 256, 260, 269, 277, 282, 283, 285, 287, 295, 305, 309, 314, 324, 329, 334, 364
  description 251
San Diego, CA 80
Saskatchewen, Canada 327, 329. *See also* bread basket
Satan 268
seamless garment 296
  definition 364
  signification 286
Sea of Ellipse: Gulf of Alaska 321
Seattle, WA 44, 48, 63
Serapis Bey 364
Service 253. *See also* Twelve Jurisdictions
  and the Rays 229
  expands the self 226
  giving without expectation 224, 231
  is born of love 225
  releases power 224
Seven Archangels 287
Seven Rays 287, 292. *See also* Ray(s)
Seventh Cycle 104, 364

Seventh Dimension 137
Seventh Manu 172
  definition 364
Shalahah
  Golden City of 54
silver cord 176
Silver Crystal Mountains: West Indies 157. *See also* Pillar Peaks
Snake Lake: Idaho, USA 73, 82
Snake River Canyon 49
soul 76, 93, 103, 115, 116, 141, 152, 261
Soul
  definition 365
soul groups 117
souls
  new 142
sound
  energy meridians in human physiology 264
South America 102, 108, 122, 124, 127, 140, 145, 170, 171, 188, 348
  holds the spark of desire for the planet 348
  once connected to Africa 129
Spiritual Awakening
  definition 365
Spiritual Hierarchy. *See also* Great White Brotherhood
  definition 365
Spokane, WA 63
sponsorship
  definition 365
Star Island: Bahamas 167
Starseed 160, 289, 306, 307
  Consiousness
    definition 365
  Thirteen 309

stillness. *See also* Twelve Jurisdictions
  and aligning 280
  and allowing 279
  and contemplation 279
  and silence 281
  and the creation process 278
  completes a cycle 279
sun
  symbol 289
symbols 290

T

Tablet Islands: Utah, USA 75, 82
Tehekoa
  Golden City of 172, 365
telepathy 84
Temple of Mercy 351
Terra
  definition 365
Texas. *See also* Harvest Bay
  new coastline 54
"The Light of God Never Fails" 72
third eye chakra 135
  definition 365
thought, feeling, and action
  definition 365
Threefold Flame 262, 268
  and energy frequencies 265
  creation of 262
Three Sisters 365
time compaction 124, 164, 339
Time of Change 124
  definition 366
Time of Transition 101, 110, 113, 149, 195
  and the Violet Flame 259
  definition 366
timing of events
  by reading earth's energy fields 339
Toronto, Ontario 349
Transportation Center: Coeur d'Alene, ID and Bismarck, ND 76, 77

Trinity Islands: Hawaii, USA 80
trust 128
tunnels 321
  Alaska and Canada 82
Twelve Jurisdictions 41, 179, 184, 188, 218, 287, 288
  as the structure or law for earth in the New Times 260
  Charity
    definition 355
  Clarity
    definition 355
  Cooperation
    definition 356
  Creation
    definition 356
  Desire
    definition 356
  Faith
    definition 358
  Illumination
    definition 360
  Love
    definition 361
  New World Constitution 221
  Service
    definition 364
  Stillness
    definition 365
Twelve Rays 289, 292. *See also* Ray(s)
twelve tribes. *See also* Chamber of Planetary Justice
  symbology 272

U

UFOs
  convention of 1991 110
  star crafts 317
Unfed Flame 309
  definition 366

United States
  climate and wind patterns 78
  divine purpose with Canada 345
  symbols in the future 62
  the new west coast 48
Unity Lake: Great Lakes, United States and Canada 66, 78, 82, 86, 342, 343, 347
Universal Law
  definition 366
Universal Principles 94
Upper Lake: Pennsylvania, USA 86
Utah 49, 53, 75

V

Vancouver, BC 48, 63, 81
Vancouver Island 63
veil 243, 248
Venus 239, 240, 246, 247, 250, 285, 295, 316, 332
victory
  Laurel of Gratitude 297. *See also* Apollo
Violet Flame 102, 119, 137, 152, 177, 179, 230, 259, 270, 294, 310, 311, 346, 351
  and Eternal Love 96
  at Sunrise and Sunset 351
  definition 366
Violet Flame Angels 294
Violet Ray 153, 214, 285, 346
Violet Sun 346
volcanic activity 112
  and new mountains in Canada 317
Vortex 47, 49, 53, 55, 60, 61, 67, 73, 87, 92, 130, 133, 145, 159, 163, 171, 176, 307, 315, 326, 340
  definition 367
Vortex Structure. *See also* Golden City Structure

W

Wahanee
  Golden City of 367
Wallowa Mountains: Oregon, USA 48
Washington D.C. 44, 61, 77
Washington State 48
water 38, 48, 49, 52, 55, 60, 63, 67, 76, 82, 107, 110, 112, 127, 140, 160, 165, 189, 194, 211, 222, 266, 320, 323, 329, 330, 333, 335, 337, 343, 347
  and healing 308
  element 111
Weather Crystal: Washington State, USA 79, 138, 326
White Dove Island: West Coast of South America; Nazca Ridge and Chile Basin, Pacific Ocean 176
will 134, 136, 169, 173, 190, 276, 309
  definition 367
Willamette Valley 79
wind
  distributes water and fire during the changes 323
wind pattern 78. *See also* weather patterns
Wyoming 44

Y

Yellowstone River 84
Yucatan 108, 112, 113, 120, 121, 129, 153, 161
Yukon 322, 323
Yuthor
  Golden City of 367

Z

Zadkiel. *See* Archangel: Zadkiel

About Lori Toye

Lori Toye is not a Prophet of doom and gloom. The fact that she became a Prophet at all is highly unlikely. Reared in a small Idaho farming community as a member of the conservative Missouri Synod Lutheran church, Lori had never heard of meditation, spiritual development, reincarnation, channeling, or clairvoyant sight.

Her unusual spiritual journey began in Washington State, when, as advertising manager of a weekly newspaper, she answered a request to pick up an ad for a local health food store. As she entered, a woman at the counter pointed a finger at her and said, "You have work to do for Master Saint Germain!"

The next several years were filled with spiritual enlightenment that introduced Lori, then only twenty-two years old, to the most exceptional and inspirational information she had ever encountered. Lori became a student of Ascended Master teachings. Awakened one night by the luminous figure of Saint Germain at the foot of her bed, her work had begun. Later in the same year, an image of a map appeared in her dream. Four teachers clad in white robes were present, pointing out Earth Changes that would shape the future United States.

Five years later, faced with the stress of a painful divorce and rebuilding her life as a single mother, Lori attended spiritual meditation classes. While there, she shared her experience, and encouraged by friends, she began to explore the dream through daily meditation. The four Beings appeared again, and expressed a willingness to share the information. Over a six-month period, they gave over eighty sessions of material, including detailed information that would later become the I AM America Map.

Clearly she had to produce the map. The only means to finance it was to sell her house. She put her home up for sale, and in a depressed market, it sold the first day at full asking price.

She produced the map in 1989, rolled copies of them on her kitchen table, and sold them through word-of-mouth. She then launched a lecture tour of the Northwest and California. Hers was the first Earth Changes Map published, and many others have followed, but the rest is history.

From the tabloids to the *New York Times*, *The Washington Post*, television interviews in the U.S., London, and Europe, Lori's Mission was to honor the material she had received. The material is not hers, she stresses. It belongs to the Masters, and their loving, healing approach is disseminated through the I AM America Publishing Company operated by her husband and spiritual partner, Lenard Toye. Working together they organized free classes of the teachings and their instructional pursuits led them to form the School of the Four Pillars which includes holistic and energy healing techniques. In 1995 and 1996 they sponsored the first Prophecy Conferences in Philadelphia and Phoenix, Arizona.

Other publications include three additional Prophecy maps, eleven books, a video, and more than sixty audio tapes based on sessions with Master Teacher Saint Germain and other Ascended Masters.

Spiritual in nature, I AM America is not a church, religion, sect, or cult. There is no interest or intent in amassing followers or engaging in any activity other than what Lori and Lenard can do on their own to publicize the materials they have been entrusted with.

They have also been directed to build the first Golden City community. A very positive aspect of the vision is that all the maps include areas called, "Golden Cities." These places hold a high spiritual energy, and are where sustainable communities are to be built using solar energy alongside classical feng shui engineering and infrastructure. The first community, Wenima Village, is currently being planned for development.

Concerned that some might misinterpret the Maps' messages as doom and gloom and miss the metaphor for personal change, or not consider the spiritual teachings attached to the maps, Lori emphasizes that the Masters stressed that this was a Prophecy of choice. Prophecy allows for choice in making informed decisions and promotes the opportunity for cooperation and harmony. Lenard and Lori's vision for I AM America is to share the Ascended Masters' prophecies as spiritual warnings to heal and renew our lives.

About I AM America

I AM America is an educational and publishing foundation dedicated to disseminating the Ascended Masters' message of Earth Changes Prophecy and Spiritual Teachings for self-development. Our office is run by the husband and wife team of Lenard and Lori Toye who hand-roll maps, package, and mail information and products with a small staff. Our first publication was the I AM America Map, which was published in September 1989. Since then we have published three more Prophecy maps, nine books, and numerous recordings based on the channeled sessions with the Spiritual Teachers.

We are not a church, a religion, a sect, or cult and are not interested in amassing followers or members. Nor do we have any affiliation with a church, religion, political group, or government of any kind. We are not a college or university, research facility, or a mystery school. El Morya told us that the best way to see ourselves is as, "Cosmic Beings, having a human experience."

In 1994, we asked Saint Germain, "How do you see our work at I AM America?" and he answered, "I AM America is to be a clearinghouse for the new humanity." Grabbing a dictionary, we quickly learned that the term "clearinghouse" refers to "an organization or unit within an organization that functions as a central agency for collecting, organizing, storing, and disseminating documents, usually within a specific academic discipline or field." So inarguably, we are this too. But in uncomplicated terms, we publish and share spiritually transformational information because at I AM America there is no doubt that, "A Change of Heart can Change the World."

With Violet Flame Blessings,
Lori & Lenard Toye

Navigating the New Earth

I AM America Map
US Earth Changes
Order #001

Freedom Star Map
World Earth Changes
Order #004

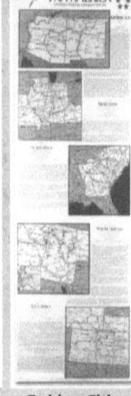

Since 1989, I AM America has been publishing thought-provoking information on Earth Changes. All of our Maps feature the compelling cartography of the New Times illustrated with careful details and unique graphics. Professionally presented in full color. Explore the prophetic possibilities!

Retail and Wholesale prices available.

Purchase Maps at:
www.IAMAMERICA.com

6-Map Scenario
US Earth Changes Progression
Order #022

Golden Cities Map
United States
Order #110

AMERICA

P.O. Box 2511
Payson, Arizona
(480) 744-6188

www.ingramcontent.com/pod-product-compliance
Lightning Source LLC
Chambersburg PA
CBHW031054080526
44587CB00011B/685